Guerrilla Creativity

Other Books by Jay Conrad Levinson

The Most Important $1.00 Book Ever Written

Secrets of Successful Free-Lancing

San Francisco: An Unusual Guide to Unusual Shopping
   (*with Pat Levinson and John Bear*)

Earning Money Without a Job

555 Ways to Earn Extra Money

150 Secrets of Successful Weight Loss (*with Michael Lavin
   and Michael Rokeach*)

Quit Your Job!

An Earthling's Guide to Satellite TV

Guerrilla Marketing

Guerrilla Marketing Attack

The Investor's Guide to the Photovoltaic Industry

Guerrilla Marketing Weapons

The 90-Minute Hour

Guerrilla Financing (*with Bruce Jay Blechman*)

Guerrilla Selling (*with Bill Gallagher and Orvel Ray Wilson*)

Guerrilla Marketing Excellence

Guerrilla Advertising

Guerrilla Marketing Handbook (*with Seth Godin*)

Guerrilla Marketing Online (*with Charles Rubin*)

Guerrilla Marketing for the Home-Based Business
   (*with Seth Godin*)

The Way of the Guerrilla

Guerrilla Trade-Show Selling (*with Mark S. A. Smith
   and Orvel Ray Wilson*)

Get What You Deserve: How to Guerrilla-Market Yourself
   (*with Seth Godin*)

Guerrilla Marketing with Technology

Guerrilla Negotiating (*with Mark S. A. Smith and Orvel
   Ray Wilson*)

Guerrilla Saving (*with Kathryn Tyler*)

Mastering Guerrilla Marketing

Guerrilla Marketing for Writers (*with Rick Frishman
   and Michael Larsen*)

Guerrilla
CREATIVITY

Make Your Message Irresistible
with the Power of Memes

Jay Conrad Levinson

Houghton Mifflin Company
Boston   New York   2001

For information about permission to reproduce selections from
this book, write to Permissions, Houghton Mifflin Company,
215 Park Avenue South, New York, New York 10003.

Visit our Web site: www.houghtonmifflinbooks.com.

Library of Congress Cataloging-in-Publication Data

Levinson, Jay Conrad.
Guerrilla creativity: make your message irresistible
with the power of memes / Jay Conrad Levinson.
     p.   cm.
Includes bibliographical references and index.
ISBN 0-618-10468-2
1. Marketing. 2. Creative ability. I. Title.
HF5415 .L4759 2001
658.8 — dc21   2001024987

Printed in the United States of America

Book design by Robert Overholtzer

QUM 10 9 8 7 6 5 4 3 2 1

The quote on pages 39–40, adapted from David Brin, "The New Meme,"
copyright © 1993 by David Brin (http://www.davidbrin.com), is reproduced by permission of the author. The quote from "'Memes' Spreading
Rapidly Across Web" by Edward Rothstein, copyright © 1996 by The
New York Times Co., is reprinted by permission. All *Advertising Age*
material is reprinted with permission from the November 1999 special
issue of *Advertising Age.* Copyright © Crain Communications Inc. 1999.
The quotes from Geoffrey Ayling, *Rapid Response Advertising,* and from
Roy H. Williams, *Secret Formulas of the Wizard of Ads,* are reproduced
by permission.

I dedicate this book to my wife, Patsy,
the Goddess of Creativity, and to my angel,
Jeannie Huffman, the Goddess of Our House.
The meme for Patsy would be children
holding an artist's palette; the meme for Jeannie
would be an artist's palette holding children.

Acknowledgments

I owe the most profound acknowledgments of all to two gentlemen who no longer grace our planet: Howard Gossage and Leo Burnett, who taught me all I know about creativity while serving as my bosses at advertising agencies that were heavens in disguise.

I'll always feel an unpaid debt of gratitude to Bill Shear, who masterminds the growth of all things guerrilla, and to Michael Larsen and Elizabeth Pomada, shepherds of my words to your hands.

Mitch Meyerson and Steve Savage knock me out with their inherent guerrilla minds, which I gratefully acknowledge here. Mark Joyner and Charlie Kessler continue to impress me with their own brand of creativity, always inspiring and enlightening to me.

My daughter, Amy, blows me away with the gale-force creativity demonstrated by the quality of her writing. I can't wait till I read the acknowledgments in the book she writes.

Finally I get to acknowledge my editor, Eamon Dolan, who recognized memes for what they are and who is helping me move them to safety from the wrist-slapping of computer spellcheckers.

Marin County, California
2001

Contents

Guerrilla Creativity

1

The Purpose of Creativity

▶ ▶ ▶ *Not Producing Art but*
Changing Human Behavior

T
HE PREHISTORIC MAN Uba spent all day in the drizzling rain trying to catch a fish because his family desperately needed food. But Uba couldn't grab a fish from the stream, though he occasionally got his hands on one. Frustrated and weak from hunger, he just couldn't grab any fish firmly enough before it slithered from his hands and returned to the stream. Worse yet, the drizzle turned to a downpour, and Uba was forced to seek shelter in a nearby cave.

When his eyes became accustomed to the dark, he noticed a series of paintings in the cave. One depicted a deer. Another showed a godlike figure.

But it was the third that captured his attention. There on the cave wall was a simple drawing of a man holding a long stick. At the end of the stick, a fish was impaled. Suddenly Uba got the idea! Within an hour he returned to his family carrying five fish, all of which he had caught with a sharpened stick. Uba's family was saved by a meme.

A meme is a self-explanatory symbol, using words, action, sounds, or, in this case, pictures that communicate an entire idea. Uba may have discovered history's first meme.

Memes can do a lot more than save a family. Memes can save a business as well and propel it into a high-profit mode. Guerrilla creativity means enlisting the wondrous power of memes in your marketing.

What you don't know about creativity

What you don't know about creativity subtracts from your potential profits every year. What you are about to learn will add to your profits — now and forever. It's something as foreign to you as the Internet was back in the 1970s — but every bit as important as the Internet is now when it comes to your company's profitability.

This book is about creativity in marketing — guerrilla creativity. Creativity in marketing is very different from creativity in the arts. Memes in marketing are about profits. And guerrilla creativity has at its core a meme. That's why the star of this book, and the key to true guerrilla creativity, is a meme.

The wheel is a meme. The Green Giant is a meme. You'll become aware of many more memes as you read on, but mainly you'll discover the astonishing lack of memes in marketing. Bad as this is, it's a great opportunity for guerrillas.

Guerrilla creativity tells you it's time for your company to have its own meme. Guerrilla creativity suggests that if you get in your prospects' faces with your meme, they will make it part of their family.

What memes do

Memes travel. Memes spread. Memes are viral. In fact, in scientific circles they're referred to as "mind viruses." Memes are simple to create. And memes can goose your company's profitability, not to mention civilization itself.

Memes save you money because they implant a message that's repeated to the point where people are clear on what you offer and you don't have to constantly change your marketing campaign. They break through the sensory overload that increases every day. The bigger that overload, the more you need a meme for your company.

Richard Dawkins, an Oxford biologist who coined the word *meme* in 1976 in his book *The Selfish Gene,* defines it as a basic unit of cultural transmission or imitation. Guerrilla marketers define it as the essence of an idea, expressed as a symbol or set of words, an action or a sound . . . or all of these.

You must know three things about the meme:

1. It's the lowest common denominator of an idea, a basic unit of communication.

2. It can alter human behavior, and in guerrilla marketing that means motivating people to buy whatever the guerrilla offers.

3. It is simplicity itself, easily understandable in a matter of seconds.

Memes make perfect partners for marketing campaigns, in which ideas must stand apart in an ocean of other ideas and be communicated instantly — or else.

Within two seconds a meme conveys who you are and why

someone should buy from you instead of a competitor. It also can trigger an emotional response and generate a desire.

Meme power

The essence of guerrilla creativity is creating marketing that has meme power. Guerrilla creativity is dreaming up a symbol or words, actions or sounds, that convey a concept anybody can understand instantly and easily.

Creativity in the arts is about enjoyment, self-expression, and beauty. Creativity in marketing is not about these aesthetic concerns but about profits, selling, motivating. Creativity in marketing is about how your product or service improves lives.

Your profits will rise if you create a simple meme for your business, then promote it for years, decades — centuries if possible.

This can be done with words (Lean Cuisine), pictures (the Marlboro cowboy), sounds (the "Ho-ho-ho" of the Jolly Green Giant), actions (Clydesdales pulling the Budweiser wagon), or imagery (flames depicting Burger King's flame-broiled hamburgers). Memes have been the architects of human behavior since the beginning of time. The wheel was a major improvement in transportation and conveyance, but it was also a meme because it was a self-explanatory symbol representing a complete idea. Once you see a wheel, you immediately know how to use it and why it's so useful. No explanation is necessary.

Where memes are born

Memes are born through knowledge and research. They work their wonders by engaging the unconscious minds of your prospects. Although they've been around since the beginning of humankind, and even since the beginning of life on earth — since life forms often leave behind meme-like signals such as half-eaten shrubbery, scat and shells, which trigger behaviors in other life forms — memes are relatively new to marketing. I know that *meme* is a new word to you, but then again, so was the word *Internet* a scant decade ago.

Right now I urge you to put aside for a moment what you think you know about creativity. Transfer your focus from the kind of creativity it takes to create beauty and splendor, symphonies and literature, dance and sculpture, and refocus on the production of profits.

Creativity in the arts enlightens, delights, moves, and satisfies. Creativity in marketing changes human behavior. Creativity that accomplishes this goal is true guerrilla creativity.

The primary purpose of guerrilla creativity is to instill enough trust and confidence in your offering that people will be motivated to purchase it — the end result being profits for your company. Yes, guerrilla creativity does employ art to accomplish the goals of business. Marketing uses nearly all the art forms — writing, art, design, music, dance, acting — but it uses them for a different purpose than that pursued by a Shakespeare or a Baryshnikov. I believe that the great masters in art, music, and literature might have been geniuses at guerrilla creativity. Still, Ernest Hemingway observed that writing advertising is a lot more difficult than writing for the pure sake of art. It does seem a lot simpler to create something that inspires a person than to create something that will persuade that same person to part with his or her hard-earned dollars.

Creativity of the guerrilla variety combines the creativity of the arts with the science of human behavior and the business of generating profits — all in a quest to get people to change their minds and sincerely want what you offer.

The purpose of guerrilla creativity

Guerrilla creativity must inform rather than entertain. In artistic creativity, an error can be covered with white paint and repainted; an error in a music composition can be rescored; an error in architecture can be covered with ivy. But an error in marketing creativity results in the loss of a lot of money. Ivy won't help.

As with creativity in the arts, guerrilla creativity entails taking risks. It embraces failure as part of the creative process if that failure teaches a valuable lesson, as it often does. Guerrilla creativity must make a deep impression on the target audience. In these pages, you'll learn how to make that impression. You'll discover how to marry it to persuasion and induce each of your prospects to participate in the marketing process.

Creativity has often been defined as the combining of two or more elements — with imagination as well as technical skill — that have never before been combined. Guerrilla marketing embraces this definition but carries it further: creativity is causing human beings to change their minds to the point where they want to purchase what you are offering to sell.

The purpose of creativity for many an artist is self-expression. Unfortunately, many who now toil in the creative departments of advertising agencies or companies also create marketing materials for the sake of self-expression, much to the dismay of those concerned with the company's bottom line.

Making the guerrilla's job easier

The job of the guerrilla who creates marketing materials is made immensely simpler when he or she enlists the power of a meme. Memes make it easier for prospects to understand why they should become customers. Uba the caveman didn't have to engage in much deep thinking before he got the point of the meme he saw in the cave. These days I view far too many television commercials and print ads that force me to engage in seriously deep thought just to determine who the heck the advertiser is, what the company makes, and why I should give it my business. The fact that I have to think so hard to grasp those commercials suggests that their creators didn't think enough about the things guerrilla marketers must know well.

The birthplace of guerrilla creativity is knowledge. The more knowledge you have, the more creative you can be. The more knowledge you have, the more inspired you can be. The more knowledge you have, the more likely you are to succeed at the true purpose of guerrilla creativity.

Where is a guerrilla to seek knowledge? From his customers, to be sure. Also from his prospects. He seeks it from his competitors, from his industry, from his community, and from the events of the day. He seeks and gains even more knowledge from the economic trends of the times, from businesses like his own, and definitely from his product or service. Certainly he seeks it from successful marketing in the past, from the current status of the media, and these days more than ever, from existing technology. The Internet is a treasure trove of knowledge for those who would engage in guerrilla creativity.

Rembrandt as a guerrilla

Do you think Rembrandt would have employed computer technology and the Internet to create his works of art? I think he would have. And so would Shakespeare and Mozart and many of the other masters of fine art. One of the keys to creativity has always been curiosity, and I can't help but believe that the creative geniuses of the past were highly curious people. My guess is that they, just like the guerrilla, had a well-honed sense of wonder. Most of them learned that the more in touch they were with the world around them, the more creative they could be.

Like the guerrilla marketer, they probably had an unquenchable and instinctive desire to learn. But nevertheless, they had it easy compared to you. You have to get people to write a check, take out their credit card, or put in a purchase order. Do that and you've earned your creative wings.

Guerrilla creativity may not unleash that creative genius said to be lurking within your mind. It may not give wings to your soul. It may not astound people with the sheer beauty of your creation. It may not inspire thoughts of love, of holiness, of the magnificence of humankind.

Those are not its tasks. Its task is to create a desire for your product or service. Beauty alone cannot accomplish this. Artistic prowess cannot either. In my career in advertising agencies, I had the singularly unpleasant task of firing many multi-talented artists and writers who were blessed with an artistic muse but totally clueless when it came to altering human behavior.

"I hate to tell you this, Mr. da Vinci, but your Mona Lisa, pretty and mysterious as she is, does no more than a hill of

beans when it comes to selling insurance. But don't worry —
I'm giving you three months' severance pay."

Had Leonardo portrayed Mona Lisa cupping her hands in
front of her to show you're in good hands with the insurance
company she was promoting, I probably would have promoted
him to senior art director.

So here I am, imploring you to understand that creativity in
marketing is quite different from creativity in the fine arts. But
I'm not going to leave you out on a limb. Instead, I'm giving
you a method, a nearly magical method, for accomplishing
guerrilla creativity. I will show you, step by step, how to create
a meme to make your job of generating profits easier, to make
your prospects' job of wanting to buy what you are selling easier, and to put a wide grin on your accountant's face when he or
she reviews your financial records.

Why genius is not necessary

*You need not be a creative whiz to exercise dynamite guerrilla
creativity.* You don't have to be a fine writer, an accomplished
artist, a killer photographer, or a superb playwright to be a successful creator of marketing that beautifies your bottom line.

All you must be is a clear thinker, a tireless researcher, and a
realistic person. You must be passionate as well, not about
beauty and art, but about your product or service. It also helps a
lot if you care more about profits than about compliments and
awards. Sound mercenary? That's my point. The pursuit of
profits has rarely, if ever, been the prime motivator for a great
artistic master. But it is the central ambition of a master of
guerrilla creativity.

Roy H. Williams, known as "the Wizard of Ads," reminds us of the differences between some writers of radio commercials. Tell 'em, Roy: "Average writers position the listener as an uninvolved bystander. Good writers position the listener as an interested observer. Great writers involve the listener as an active participant." To this I would add: "Guerrilla writers motivate the listener to deeply crave whatever it is they are writing about."

Guerrilla writers know how to instill trust and confidence in the minds of their audience. They create marketing that doesn't really sound or feel like marketing.

The heart of a message

Creativity of the guerrilla persuasion has as its final message something that deeply impresses the audience. They are not impressed with the words or the pictures, with the music or the special effects. They are not impressed with the celebrity endorser or the eye-popping photograph. Instead, they are deeply impressed with the idea. Uba didn't grunt one word about the art in the meme he discovered in that cave. But he was moved to take action by the *idea*. That's always the highlight of a guerrilla marketing message. If you don't communicate an idea, you're communicating the wrong things. You'll always find persuasion at the heart of a message created by a guerrilla.

Guerrillas know that *marketing* is a fancy word that means selling, and *selling* is a fancy word that means persuasion. If you can't persuade, you can't sell. If you can't sell, you can't market. Persuasion is a crucial talent if you have a business and a fondness for the things that money can buy.

Many people who think they can't succeed at marketing because they can't persuade seem to do a dandy job of persuading their spouse to be on time, their kids to do their homework, and their associates to accept the idea they've just put on the table. The moral? There are a lot of closet persuaders out there, and you're probably one of them.

Guerrillas rev up their powers of persuasion with two kinds of insight: insight into their prospects and customers combined with insight into their own product or service. Without those insights, you're a dead duck. With them, you're a guerrilla, poised for victory and profitability.

Whom to persuade?

So whom should you persuade? That may be the toughest question your business must answer. The right answer can lead to the attainment of your wildest dreams — and you don't have to tell me how wild those dreams are. But when you know who it is you are going to persuade, you are only part of the way home. You must also know what is important to them.

Here's a flash: persuasion can be straightforward. Most business owners, and even those who create marketing for them, think that persuading has a lot to do with pussyfooting around and playing needless games. Even if they know exactly whom they should be persuading, they don't know the hot buttons that ignite that person. No wonder they're pussyfooting! There's not a lot to be candid about.

I'm the first to admit that not every persuasion attempt you make will work out the way you want. But I'm here in these pages to remind you to realize why some attempts succeed, to realize why some fail, and to recognize the difference between the two.

Guerrillas ask themselves questions after successful persuasions. "What was the critical insight that I used?" and, "How did I use it?" Of failures, they ask: "What insight should I have seen?" and, "How did my attempt miss it?"

Frequently, failures are caused by persuaders failing to understand the person they are attempting to persuade. The deeper you probe into the head of your prospect, the more persuasive you will become because of the broader scope of your understanding.

Within that understanding resides your power of persuasion, your guerrilla creativity. If you become a better persuader, you become a better salesperson. If you become a better salesperson, you become a better marketer. You become a guerrilla — one who achieves conventional goals with unconventional methods.

Just ask Uba

Guerrilla persuasion is knowing your customers and prospects so well that it's a cinch to connect their goals with yours. Just ask Uba. He'll tell you. So now you know the truth. There is no magic in persuasion. There is simply research time and your own energy.

Back in the 1900s, the ad great Claude Hopkins said — and I hope you'll excuse his sexism — "The advertising man studies the consumer. He tries to place himself in the position of the buyer. His success largely depends on doing that to the exclusion of everything else." The keys to persuasion are in shoes and eyes. Walk a mile in your customer's shoes and see things through his eyes.

Guerrilla persuading and guerrilla creativity mean connecting intimately with consumers. The connection begins in your own mind — and it continues until a sale is made. Gentle persuasion can be as powerful as pressured persuasion. Slow-motion persuasion works better than high-speed persuasion. I don't have to remind you who won the race between that swift hare and that plodding tortoise. And I'm pretty sure you understand that all persuasion begins with connection. Knowing that, all that remains is for you to know what to be creative about. And that's just what you'll learn in the next chapter.

2

What to Be Creative About

▶ ▶ ▶ *Your Offering Can Make Lives Better*

THERE'S A WHOLE LOT of creativity out there, especially in the marketing arena, but it's being used for the wrong things. Here's the problem: the advertising world is filled with people younger than their audience. Those younger people seem to be embarrassed that they are creating advertising, so they do everything they can to make their creations look and feel like anything but an ad.

They are extremely successful at creating nonadvertising advertising, but that's not where they ought to be directing their genius. The ads and commercials they create are fascinating to see, and delightful to read, but woeful as sales tools. That's because they are creative about things other than the product or service they are hawking. Hawking? I think most American creative types would blanch at the very thought that they are hawking anything. Yet my dictionary defines *hawking* as carrying goods for sale, and that's what creative types should be doing. They are engaged in salesmanship, not a masquerade party.

The price isn't right

Judging by much of the marketing you see every day, you'd think that the thing to be creative about is price. Let me tell you here and now — marketing people focus on price only when their well has run dry and they are seeking the refuge of the highly uncreative. How many product categories in America are led by the lowest-priced brand? The answer is: zero. How much profit is there in offering the lowest-priced product? The answer is: barely more than zero. This strategy is hardly the cornerstone for a successful business.

The truth is that people don't care about price nearly as much as they care about value. If you're offering the cheapest widget in the land and a competitive widget costs twice as much but lasts ten times longer, you can count on people going for that higher-priced widget because of the value it offers. There is a whole lot of latitude for guerrilla creativity if you're going to be creative about the value of your offering. But if it's merely price you'll be stressing, I'll wager my money on your competitor — and I'll give you odds.

Gillette's Mach3 razor debuted at a 50 percent premium price over the most expensive razor blade available at the time, and it quickly became the number-one brand on the market, taking Gillette to its highest market share in a decade. Colgate introduced its Total toothpaste at a 23 percent premium price, and in less than a year it became the top seller. Maytag — the company whose lonely repairman has been lonely for longer than most businesses have been in operation — introduced the Neptune washing machine at twice the cost of conventional washing machines, and it almost immediately became the number-two seller in America.

Abundant opportunities for guerrilla creativity reside in an offering's novelty. Some who create marketing materials shy away from positioning their offering as new because they figure people are scared to death of something untried, unproven, and unpopular. Others are so excited at the chance to announce something new that they aim all their guns at the newness.

Students of both of these schools get a failing grade from this guerrilla. A new product or service has built-in excitement because many people are attracted to new things. But newness itself is hardly a marketing strategy. If what you offer is new, I encourage you to shout it from the rafters, but while you're shouting, be certain to explain why it is good and how it will make a life or a business better — why it gives hope. If it's new and that's all, you'll get a big ho-hum. If it's new and it increases profits or saves time, you'll get rapt attention.

While doing research for this book, which I've been doing since 1958, I've generally been appalled at what those who create marketing select as the focus of their creativity. Many of them start out in the wrong direction. In the work of many others, I can't for the life of me spot their focal point. To many marketing people, the thing to be creative about is the marketing message. My words of wisdom to these people: *Forget the marketing. Make the product or service interesting. That's where true guerrilla creativity is born.*

Where to focus your creativity

Be creative about what you are offering, not in your manner of marketing it. Be creative about your audience, about their fears, their worries, their wants, their desires, their dreams, their insecurities, their opportunities — but not in your method of marketing.

Be creative in your efforts to develop your offering and about the great things it provides, about the ways it enhances lives, about the research you did before you brought it to market, about the quality it provides — but not in the way you've decided to promote it.

Here's a home truth that may hurt your feelings but should make up for the pain with enlightenment. When a survey was conducted to determine how people feel about marketing, it revealed that *people don't really care about marketing; most of them have never even given it a thought.* Marketing to most people is something to ignore, as meaningless as a gnat on a windshield, or a single raindrop in a rainstorm.

The whole world is not waiting

In assessing current marketing, it seems to me that many people who create marketing think the whole world is waiting for their message. I'm here to tell you that the whole world is looking the other way and that deep in their hearts they are hoping you'll remain silent and let them get on with their lives. Those lives have very little connection with marketing. Yes, yes, yes, I know how important marketing is to your company. Mine too. But the rest of Planet Earth is on a totally different wavelength. Stop marketing and see how many letters of complaint you receive. One letter? Gee, that's far more than I expected.

Hardly anybody except for marketing mavens such as myself decide to spend an evening studying TV commercials, reading online banners, poring over ads, reading brochures, listening to radio commercials, or cozying up to a bevy of direct-mail letters. I do admit that my own wife thinks an exciting evening is one spent perusing catalogs, but I guarantee that she is an exception to my rule. And I urge you to leave her alone already. She has enough catalogs. I also admit that my dog's tail wags in delight when the UPS truck pulls up in the driveway as a result of my wife's catalogism. He thinks each box delivered by the UPS man or woman is carrying tennis balls for his recreation or steaks for his culinary enjoyment. But he is wrong, wrong, wrong. And so are you if you think your target audience has a lot in common with my wife or my puppy.

Because of the near-universal apathy toward marketing, I hope you don't make yours even more typical. If there is anything to be creative about when it comes to your offering, it's the unexpected. Surprise people. Tell them what they don't already know and haven't already heard umpteen times. If you surprise them, even shock them, at least you've got a good chance of capturing their attention. But you won't capture it if you say what they expect you to say and they hope you won't say again.

With so much poorly focused marketing bombarding your prospects, you're sure to surprise them if you focus on the ideas and emotions I'm about to reveal in this chapter. They need your focus and your creativity.

Five areas begging for creativity

Ironically, there are loads of things about which marketers can and should be creative. For openers, here are the five key areas just begging for their creativity:

1. The problems faced by their target audience.

2. The ways their offering can solve the problems of their target audience.

3. The other benefits offered by their product or service.

4. The drama inherent in whatever they are selling. All products and services have at least one element of inherent drama, such as Folger's coffee being grown in the mountains. All coffee happens to be grown in the mountains, but Folger's was the first coffee maker to say "mountain-grown," capitalizing on the product's inherent drama

5. The unique features of their offering. That could be a long list, but remember that people buy benefits more than they buy features. Unibody construction may be the feature of a car, but silent vehicle operation is the benefit. Aluminum chlorohydrate may be the feature of an antiperspirant, but stopping perspiration is the benefit.

Let's take a moment to examine all five areas so as to add fuel to the fires burning within the hearts of those who create marketing.

1. *The problems facing your target audience are very meaningful to them.* They are dying for a solution. If you exercise your creativity to present them with a solution, you're far more likely to win their attention, not to mention their business. Do they care daily about your widget? You know they don't. Do they care daily about that spare tire around their waistline or the sparse numbers on their bottom line? Yes, they do. They care about those problems morning, noon, and night. Sometimes these problems keep them up all night. If you can provide

them with a solution through what you are selling to them, you're talking their language and they care about what you say. If it comes to them in the form of advertising, who cares? All they care about is doing away with their problem.

2. *The ways in which a product or service can solve a problem represent a superb bull's-eye for guerrilla creativity.* Speak to people about their lives, not about your offering. Talk to them about how their lives can be better — by making more money, attracting a mate, saving time, losing weight, having more fun — and not about your widget. People couldn't care less about your widget, but everyone is fascinated when the topic is their own lives, their own problems, their own opportunities. It's not very difficult to be creative about the concerns of human beings. It's pretty darned hard to be creative about your widget — even if it has ten bells and eleven whistles on it.

3. *The other benefits offered by a product or service can often serve as the starting point for creativity in marketing.* People do not buy shampoo. Instead, they buy beautiful hair. People do not buy aspirin. They buy freedom from their headache. People do not buy cell phones. They purchase convenience. The meaning: people are not interested in your product or service. They are intensely interested in themselves and in what your product or service might do for them. There's loads of room for creativity in that area.

4. *Every product or service ever put up for sale has something within it that is inherently dramatic.* You use ingredients from Peru? Fascinating! You put your service team through a ten-week training course? Tell me more. You tested your software with fifty companies, all of which raved about it? That's

very dramatic. Center your creativity on that inherent drama, and you'll find that your creativity sprouts wings and flies. Best of all, it flies in the right direction — toward advancing the sale.

5. *The unique features of your offering are frequently the birthplace of guerrilla creativity.* You actually traveled to Denmark to examine firsthand the technology used on beds manufactured there? You learned that slats provide healthier back support than box springs? So you incorporated slats into your own bed design to provide that healthy support to your own customers. That's a unique feature and a positive benefit on which you can hang your hat, direct your creativity, and focus your message. Nobody else offers it but you. How can your marketing be anything but intriguing and creative when you relate that story?

Getting down to the basics

I'm dying to talk to you about memes, but I'll save that for the next chapter because there are some basic facts to understand before you rise to the challenge of creating a meme for your company.

To put your guerrilla creativity into hyperspeed, it's crucial that you know the real reasons why people make purchases. There are many reasons actually, but some sort of emotion lies beneath most of them. The fact to face is that it's exceptionally difficult to sell anything to anybody unless you tap into an emotion that they're already experiencing. Once you understand that emotion, it's fairly simple to be a master of guerrilla creativity.

Fifty reasons why people buy

Geoff Ayling, in his superb book *Rapid Response Advertising,* provides wanna-be guerrillas with a full fifty reasons why people buy. There are really far more than fifty, but I have a feeling that these fifty will get your creative juices flowing. People make purchases for these reasons, among many others:

1. To make more money — even though it can't buy happiness

2. To become more comfortable, even a bit more

3. To attract praise — because almost everybody loves it

4. To increase enjoyment — of life, of business, of virtually anything

5. To possess things of beauty — because they nourish the soul

6. To avoid criticism — which nobody wants

7. To make their work easier — a constant need to many people

8. To speed up their work — because people know that time is precious

9. To keep up with the Joneses — there are Joneses in everybody's lives

10. To feel opulent — a rare, but valid reason to make a purchase

11. To look younger — owing to our culture's reverence toward youthfulness

12. To become more efficient — because efficiency saves time

13. To buy friendship — I didn't know it was for sale, but it often is

14. To avoid effort — because nobody loves to work too hard

15. To escape or avoid pain — an easy path to making a sale

16. To protect their possessions — because they worked hard to get them

17. To be in style — because few people enjoy being out of style

18. To avoid trouble — because trouble is never a joy

19. To access opportunities — because they open the doors to good things

20. To express love — one of the noblest reasons to make any purchase

21. To be entertained — because entertainment is usually fun

22. To be organized — because order makes life simpler

23. To feel safe — because security is a basic human need

24. To conserve energy — their own or their planet's sources of energy

25. To be accepted — because that means security as well as love

26. To save time — because they know time is more valuable than money

27. To become more fit and healthy — seems to me that's an easy sale

28. To attract the opposite sex — never underestimate the power of love

29. To protect their family — tapping into another basic human need

30. To emulate others — because the world is teeming with role models

31. To protect their reputation — because they worked hard to build it

32. To feel superior — which is why status symbols are sought after

33. To be trendy — because they know their friends will notice

34. To be excited — because people need excitement in a humdrum life

35. To communicate better — because they want to be understood

36. To preserve the environment — giving rise to cause-related marketing

37. To satisfy an impulse — a basic reason behind a multitude of purchases

38. To save money — the most important reason to 14 percent of the population

39. To be cleaner — because being unclean is often associated with being unhealthy and unloved

40. To be popular — because inclusion beats exclusion every time

41. To gratify curiosity — it killed the cat but motivates the sale

42. To satisfy their appetite — because hunger is not a good thing

43. To be an individual — because all of us are, and some of us need assurance

44. To escape stress — need I explain?

45. To gain convenience — because simplicity makes life easier

46. To be informed — because it's no joy to be perceived as ignorant

47. To give to others — another way people nourish their souls

48. To feel younger — because that equates with vitality and energy

49. To pursue a hobby — because all work and no play, etc., etc., etc.

50. To leave a legacy — because that's a way to live forever

There is one more area about which you should be creative, one more reason that motivates people to make a purchase, and that area deals with pain. Thomas Jefferson said, "The art of life is the art of avoiding pain; and he is the best pilot, who steers clearest of the rocks and shoals with which it is beset." More recently, Sam Deep and Lyle Sussman, who wrote *Close the Deal,* have taught the importance of pain and the ways to learn where it resides. If you know exactly where it is, you've got a heckuva great starting point for your creativity.

The pain of it all

Your customers gain confidence in you because they see you as a doctor who can ease, even eliminate, their pain. That pain sets up roadblocks to their success. To prove how your offering removes roadblocks, you've got to learn exactly what each prospect's roadblocks are.

As you hear the prospect's words, listen for the pain. Once you understand the nature and magnitude of that pain, you can work to find a cure — in your product or service.

Pain is harbored even by a prospect who believes himself or herself to be well. You must ask questions that help the prospect discover where it hurts. If you can help uncover a number of sources of pain, their totality will appear to both of you as a full-fledged illness.

Here are some questions you might ask: "Is there anything about your current situation that you don't like?" "If you could change one thing, what would it be?" "What has worked for you and what hasn't?" "If you could wave a magic wand to solve your problems, what would it do?" "How do you see me as helping you?"

Healing miracles performed here

Next, perform a healing miracle. Keep your radar carefully tuned to what your prospect is telling you, and you'll learn that his or her buying motive falls into one of seven categories:

1. *Ending present pain.* This is the most important pain to identify. It is also the one to go after first. "How much money do you think you are losing as we speak?"

2. *Avoiding future pain.* Fear of an impending outcome is also a motivator to buy, but it isn't as strong as pain in the present. "How much do you expect this problem to grow once your staff doubles in size?"

3. *Desire for pleasure in the present.* This particular item comes in third. It's your prospect's desire to gain right now, this very moment. "How much further ahead of your competitors do you wish you were?"

4. *Desire for pleasure in the future.* Delayed gratification is not as compelling as immediate gratification. To succeed with it, you need some kind of track record with your prospect. "What kind of an increase in return on investment are you looking for next year?"

5. *Avoiding a recurrence of past pain.* Prospects almost always want to avoid repeating a mistake they made before. "How would you like to never have to worry about that happening again?"

6. *Regaining past pleasure.* Prospects may want to return to their days of past glory. "How important is it for you to regain the prominence you've lost?"

7. *Interest, arousal, or curiosity.* These are the weakest motives to connect with, and yet many nonguerrillas place great stock in them. "Would you like to see something that will knock your socks off?" Although weak, these motives are the easiest to generate, as Seth Godin describes in his wonderful book *Permission Marketing,* discussed in more detail in chapter 9.

Remember that every pain your prospect feels is an opportunity for you. Remember also that your job is to uncover that pain and help the prospect to see how your offering can ease it. While interviewing or researching your prospect, keep an eye peeled for evidence of the developments you'll find in the two lists below:

Pain is felt by your prospect when these decline:

Revenues

Market share

Profit

Stock price

Shareholder value

Credit rating

Customer satisfaction

Raw materials quality

Maintenance quality

Product quality

Employee quality

Employee morale

Employee productivity

Employee accountability

Teamwork and coordination

Quality of facility management

Employee involvement

Commitment

Pain is felt by your prospect when these increase:

Raw material costs

Facility management costs

Maintenance costs

Labor costs

Employee grievances

Staff turnover

Interpersonal conflict

Interteam conflict

Accident/injury rate

Resistance to change

Missed deadlines

Inventory shrinkage

Competitor capability

Customer defections

Guerrillas are superb pain-spotters and pain-reducers. Listen for the *ouch*. The more clearly it rings in your ears, the more clearly you can see what to be creative about.

You and only you

If you've read any of my other guerrilla books, you know how much I love one-word answers. For example, if there is one word that is the secret of successful marketing, that word is *commitment*. If there is one word that describes the personality of a successful guerrilla, that word is *patient*.

And if there is one word to serve as the springboard for true guerrilla creativity, a single word that tells you plain and simple what to be creative about, that word is *you*. It should be the focal point of all your creativity. It is the starting place, the heart of the matter, and the ending point. It's what people are most interested in by far.

Many marketers create their marketing under the ridiculous

assumption that prospects are asking, "Who are you? What is your product or service? When are you open? Where are you located?" The only real question in the prospect's mind is, "Why should I care?"

Here's what they're thinking. It's not, "Tell me a story about you." Instead, it's, "Tell me a story about me. Tell me how you can save me time. Tell me how you can increase my income. Tell me how you can reduce my stress. Tell me how you can bring more love into my life. And be certain to tell me how you can cause people to think more highly of me."

You, you, you

The way to let prospects know that you are thinking about them is by saying "you" as frequently as you can. When you say "you," they know you are talking about them and not about yourself.

So you've got their attention. They want to learn more. "This is about me? I want to read about me. I want to know about me. I want to do better things for me." It's not a bear of a job to be creative when you're talking about an individual to that individual. "You want to talk about me? I'll listen to every single thing you say because, to be honest, I am plumb fascinated by myself."

Of course, if creativity were simple enough to be boiled down to one word, there would be no need for this book. Creativity is more complex than that — as you'll glean when you learn what Charles Revson, founder of Revlon, has to say about the subject. When he was asked what he sells, he came up with a splendid one-word answer: "Hope."

Hope is the product and the service

That's your cue to search for the hope that you are offering your customers. You may think you are offering a product or a service. But deep beneath the surface, we both know you are offering hope. Your job is to focus on that hope in your marketing, though I hope you do not need to use the word itself. The wildly successful Mr. Revson probably could have substituted the word *beauty* or *attractiveness* or even the phrase *sex appeal,* but all along he was marketing hope — and every member of his audience knew it in their hearts. Yes, they purchased lipstick or face powder, but they were paying their good money for hope. Who would have ever thought that hope costs less than five bucks? Charles Revson did. And so, I hope, do you.

Knowing that, you've got an even better fix on what to be creative about. Be creative about the hopes of your prospects. That's what guerrillas do. Knock yourself out showing your audience exactly what hope your offering provides and how it delivers.

What all your prospects have

Here's what all of your prospects have: an imagination. Here's what your job as a creator of marketing is: fire up that imagination. Ignite it with truth. Pour more fuel on it by talking to prospects about their favorite topic — themselves. They're more imaginative than you may figure, and it is not a Herculean task to tap into that imagination and let it ponder how your offering will add good things to their lives.

As the advertising wizard Roy Williams reminds us, "Engage the imagination, then take it where you will. Where the mind has repeatedly journeyed, the body will surely follow. People go only to places they have already been in the minds." You'd be wise to heed the words of any wizard, especially Roy.

If you're marketing things to people in business, never forget that every single one of them has a life beyond business. Every single of one of them is a person first and a businessperson next. They are multidimensional beings and may be approached with a variety of methods. Talking business is not the only method.

Consider yourself. You're the same person at work as you are at home. You're the same person in a business setting as you are in a social setting. Oh, you may discuss different topics, but your heart and soul accompany you on your daily commute. The same is true for all of your prospects. I tell you this because people involved in business-to-business marketing often fail to see their prospects as humans.

Creativity and interactivity

One of your most important tasks when determining what to be creative about is to consider the concept of interactivity. Although I'm tempted to laud the marketing powers of the Internet at this point, I'll restrain myself, because if interactivity is the true difference between offline and online marketing, what I'm referring to here is the interactivity between your marketing and your prospects.

Create marketing that makes each prospect a participant in the marketing process. Make it easy for that person to see why he or she should incorporate your offering into his or her own life. How the heck can you do this? I just told you: fire up the imaginations of your prospects. Take them places they've long dreamed of being in. When you do that, you'll be my kind of guerrilla.

Now that we're totally immersed in the reality of marketing and creativity, it is time to delve into the magic power of memes to add zest to your marketing and beauty to your bottom line.

3

The New Key to Creativity

▶ ▶ ▶ *Understanding
the Omnipotent Meme*

O NE OF YOUR MOST daunting tasks as a marketer is
to *make it easy for people to remember who you are
and why they should buy what you are selling.* If your
prospects and customers have to stop and figure out what
you're trying to say, forget it. They're not going to take that
time or expend that energy, so your message most likely won't
penetrate their inner mind, where purchase decisions are made.

That's why you need a meme. Your meme tells who you are,
helps people remember your name, and expresses instantly
why they should buy from you.

With a powerful meme, you'll actually be able to *reduce
your marketing budget* because your communications can be
more concise and economical. A meme will provide your company with a single symbol or set of words or actions that is the
essence of clarity.

It's important to know the derivation and special properties
of the word *meme,* which was created in a biological context,

though in this book we'll be dealing with memes strictly in a marketing sense. The Oxford biologist Richard Dawkins, in *The Selfish Gene,* was searching for a noun that would convey the idea of a unit of cultural transmission, a unit of imitation. First, he looked at the word *mimeme,* a Greek word meaning "something imitated," but being from the school of genetics, he wanted a monosyllabic word that sounded like *gene.* So he shortened *mimeme* to *meme.* The word looks like, and seems to relate to, the word *mime,* because of the idea of imitation. Although it does relate to memory and to the French word *même,* which means "the same," it should be pronounced to rhyme with *cream.*

Coined by Dawkins back in 1976, the word *meme* now appears in the fourth edition of the *American Heritage Dictionary,* where it is defined as: "a unit of cultural information, such as a cultural practice or idea, that is transmitted verbally or by repeated action from one mind to another." The word now also appears in the *Oxford English Dictionary,* which defines it as: "a self-replicating element of culture, passed on by imitation."

What the master memeologist says about memes

Here's what Dawkins himself has to say about memes:

> I think a new kind of replicator has recently emerged on this very planet. It is staring us in the face. It is still in its infancy, still drifting clumsily about in its primeval soup, but already is achieving evolutionary change at a rate that leaves the old gene panting far behind.
>
> The new soup is the soup of human culture.

Dawkins furnishes us with examples of memes, the "new kind of replicator," such as tunes, ideas, catchphrases, clothing fashions, and ways of making pots or building arches. He points out that as genes propagate themselves in the gene pool by leaping from body to body through sperm-egg interactions, memes propagate themselves by leaping from brain to brain through a process that might be termed "imitation." If a scientist, for example, comes across a great idea, he passes it on to his colleagues and students, both in conversations and in lectures.

If an idea catches on, it seems to propagate itself, spreading from brain to brain. Some memes, he points out, spread rapidly but don't last very long — such as popular songs and stiletto heels, pet rocks and one-hit rock stars. The best memes created for marketing spread rapidly and last a long time, such as Betty Crocker and the Budweiser Clydesdales.

Show me the money!

Tempting as it is to explore memes by delving further into genes and the whole field of genetics, that information won't do much to generate profits for your company. But the memes I intend to investigate here are entirely devoted to helping you earn those profits. And if you go about your business of guerrilla creativity, they will do just that.

Because of their extreme simplicity and self-explanatory nature, memes seem to slip into the mind and create instant understanding. That's why they're so desirable for a marketing campaign. Remember: a meme should be created as a self-explanatory item that communicates a complete idea.

When Uba the caveman spotted that meme drawn on the cave wall, he was responding to a visual meme. Memes do not always have to be visual, however. What is most crucial is that they be able to influence your prospects' buying decisions. That's where (to use a verbal meme) the rubber meets the road.

Mental software

Just as your computer software orchestrates the operation of your computer, a meme is mental software that orchestrates human behavior. Geoff Ayling explains that in the context of marketing, a meme is an idea or concept that has been refined, distilled, stripped down to its bare essentials, then super-simplified in such a way that almost anybody can grasp its meaning instantly and effortlessly.

Memes might take the form of pictures, words, sounds, symbols, or actions — individually or in combination with each other. Because they are so self-explanatory, no effort is required to grasp their meaning. Owing to that extreme simplicity, a meme enters the mind without our conscious awareness and plants a thought there.

When Nike says, "Just do it!" — is that a meme? I don't think so. Nike spends millions and millions telling us to just do it, and yet the brand does not spring to mind when you read that line, and neither does the reason to purchase the brand. Lesson: expenditures of millions of dollars do not create a meme. More than money is needed. And if you have the right meme, not much money will be required. As much as I respect the Nike marketing campaign, as a meme, in my mind, the swoosh swucks.

How long do you have?

Ask yourself: How long do I have to attract a prospect's attention? If you're marketing through radio, television, a print ad, or a Web site, the answer is: between one and three seconds. That's all. With a meme, you can convey who you are and why someone should buy from you, and you can do it lickety-split or faster.

Great memes, such as the skull-and-crossbones representing danger or the Pillsbury Doughboy representing easy baking, actually create an involuntary shift in our perception. This gives rise to an attitude that creates a change in our behavior — the ultimate goal of all marketing.

Marketing is the art and science of getting people to change their minds. Memes make that job considerably easier.

Where today's marketing misses the mark

Much of marketing today is created to win awards, plump up a creative person's ego, make the client feel good, or dazzle people with cleverness. Good marketing, however, should be created to produce a positive response in the mind of the consumer. That's why I'm going to egg you on to create your own meme. I don't care much for industry awards, people's egos, client desires, or razzle-dazzle. But I care intensely about helping you achieve a sharp upturn in your profits. Every word I write here is designed to help you accomplish just that.

Like kangaroos and frogs, like Michael Jordan and Olympic divers, memes are capable of *leaping*. They leap into the human mind from the Web site, from the magazine ad, from the

TV commercial. If your meme doesn't leap, if it doesn't convey its message instantly, it's probably not much of a meme.

The five original memes

The memeologist David Brin, in an article called "The New Meme," looks at memes from a different perspective, one that puts memes into a historic perspective and sheds more light on the meme that I'm hoping you'll create. He says:

> Let me suggest that until recently, five major memes have battled over the future of this planet . . . They are deep, old themes, which continue to set the tone for entire civilizations even today.
>
> Feudalism is one of the oldest. It may appear to be rare nowadays, but some philosophers and historians have called it the "most natural" of human societies, simply because it cropped up in so many places throughout the millennia . . .
>
> Machismo is another powerful worldview — the leading meme — in many parts of today's world. Wherever women are stifled and vengeance is touted as a primary virtue, wherever skill and craftsmanship are downgraded in favor of "strutting" and male-bonded loyalty groups, it's a good bet machismo sets the agenda . . .
>
> Then there's paranoia, another venerable family of memes. For example, one can understand the Russian tradition of xenophobia, given their history of suffering terrible invasions, on average twice a century. Still, that worldview of dour suspicion and bludgeoning distrust made for a brittle, capricious superpower, worsened by a deluding, superficial dogma, communism. If paranoia had won, or even lasted much longer, the world would probably have become a cinder sooner or later . . .
>
> The fourth worldview, which I call "The East," is one zeitgeist that is demonstrably both traditional and sane, after its fashion.

During most of recorded history it was dominant on this planet . . .

Humans might even slowly, eventually, get out into space. But when or if we ever meet aliens, we would not understand them. Because by then the very notion of diversity, let alone the idea of finding it attractive, will have been extinguished . . .

"Calm" is the last word you would use to describe the fifth meme, one that has always been a lesser theme, carried by an eccentric minority in each culture — until ours . . . It is a strange, rebellious worldview unlike any of its predecessors. One that actually encourages an appetite for newness, hunger for diversity, eagerness for change. Tolerance plays a major role in the legends spread by this new culture, plus a tradition of humorous self-criticism.

These five memes are the oldest and among the most successful of all memes, even though there are no visual symbols of feudalism, machismo, paranoia, the East, and "an appetite for newness."

One of the most powerful and ancient memes in history is the wheel. A wagon with spoked wheels not only carries freight from place to place but conveys the unmistakable idea of itself from mind to mind. Many other nonmarketing memes have made their way into our culture. The Hula-Hoop, snow-boarding, roller-blading, miniskirts, Beatle haircuts, bottled water — a long list of concepts such as these seem to roar through the community like a brushfire.

A meme may have been responsible for saving our planet. When the atomic bomb was detonated, coverage in the print media might not have communicated its power and devastating effects. But because the mushroom cloud was shown on television over and over again, much of the world was able to see and understand its destructiveness, leading to a strong anti-bomb sentiment everywhere. The meme of that mushroom cloud may be why I'm still here to write this and you're still here to read it.

When our astronauts took a photo of Earth from outer space, everyone was able to gaze at the image of that blue marble and realize that we're a single entity, and not a very large one at that.

Flowers placed in gun barrels served as a poignant meme for peace during the Vietnam war.

Computer icons are memes. I have an icon of a trashcan on my screen right now. Without any explanation I know what it means.

Memes and beliefs

Even the word *God* is a meme, because it reduces an enormous idea down to a single word, which represents the entire concept of belief in a supreme being. To understand memes even better, consider how Ayling compares memes with beliefs:

1. Beliefs are feelings of certainty about what something means. Memes are sources of information that created that feeling of certainty.

2. Beliefs are effects. Memes are causes.

3. Beliefs are attitudes that spring from ideas. Memes are simplified representations of ideas.

4. Beliefs are feelings or inclinations. Memes are basically icons with an implied subtext.

5. Beliefs are internal. Memes are external until they replicate. When they do, they become internalized and develop into beliefs.

6. Beliefs can last a lifetime and might take a while to enter a mind. Memes invade the mind in an instant and don't necessarily last a lifetime. In marketing, however, they ought to be created to last a lifetime.

7. Beliefs are expanded attitudes about life. Memes are compressed and transmissible packets of information.

8. Beliefs usually take a while to grasp entirely. Memes are the quickest and most effective ways to transmit complex concepts from one mind to another.

9. Beliefs require conscious consideration. Memes are transmitted in a moment.

For memes to become contagious, which should be the goal of those who create memes for their business, Ayling tells us that three factors are necessary:

1. *Extreme simplicity* — transmitting the core message. When you see an ad for Maxell tape, you see a man listening to his sound system, his hair and tie flying back as though he's facing a strong wind. This meme communicates that something powerful is coming from his sound system. Then Maxell lets viewers know that the something powerful is the quality of the recording tape.

2. *Emotional impact* — getting people to feel the message internally. In the last chapter, I explored the power of emotions in marketing. You see a commercial showing a woman being given a gift by her guy and her eyes misting up. Then you hear the line, "A diamond is forever," and you can't help but feel the tug on your heartstrings. Score one point for De Beers.

3. *Critical mass* — exposing enough people to the meme to spread it. How many people is enough to constitute critical mass? It depends on the product being marketed. But rather than looking for a number, look instead for a trend. If the number of people using your product or service continues to grow, you may be heading toward critical mass. Hotmail grew a subscriber base more rapidly than any company in the history of the world . . . faster than any new online, Internet, or print publication ever. Today Hotmail is the largest e-mail provider in the world. In its first one and a half years, Hotmail signed up more than twelve million subscribers. Yet, from company launch to twelve million users (now thirty million), Hotmail spent less than $500,000 on marketing, advertising, and promotion. By contrast, Juno, Hotmail's closest competitor with a fraction of the users, spent more than $20 million. The marketing meme used by Hotmail? Get your free e-mail at Hotmail. That's it. How simple can you get?

Hotmail used what is now known as "viral marketing," but the key to viral marketing is the quality of the message you wish to spread. Free e-mail is something whose perceived quality is very high. But not everything can be marketed with viral marketing.

"Viral" is the newest buzzword to hit e-mail marketing. Everyone wants his or her marketing message to be viral, and everyone wants to capitalize on viral marketing. But do people understand what it is that makes their marketing message worthy of being passed along?

During recent conference calls I had with clients, viral marketing was identified as a campaign objective right alongside "e-commerce" and "branding." Or it was mentioned as an afterthought: "Oh, and we'd like the campaign to be viral." Kind of like going through the fast-food drive-through and remembering at the end of the order: "Oh, and we want it kiddie size."

Viral marketing is not an objective: it's an integral part of a campaign strategy that is used to achieve the real objectives. It is not an add-on. You should craft your message in such a manner that it encourages pass-along.

Producing a message with a quality offer or an incentive for pass-along is what viral marketing is all about. Merely suggesting that e-mail recipients forward your message to others is not viral marketing. Adding a line at the bottom of your e-mail that reads, "Feel free to forward this message to a friend," is not viral marketing at its best.

Offer something worthy of sharing — a valuable discount or some vital information — or offer an incentive for sharing — additional entries in a sweepstakes or an added discount or premium service — and viral marketing happens naturally . . . and often quite successfully.

The bottom line is that the message must be perceived as having value.

Examples of potential pass-along material include relevant or timely information and research findings. Interactive content like a quiz or test can inspire forwarding, especially if it's fun.

Personality tests, fitness quizzes, and compatibility questionnaires have all been passed to my inbox at one time or another. Why? Because they're entertaining. And entertainment has value.

But the truth is that viral marketing is a strategy, and an integral element of your offer. It is a tactic that works toward achieving your campaign objectives, not one of your actual objectives. Incorporate this knowledge into your e-mail campaigns.

Marketing can easily deliver one, two, or all three of the factors that make a meme contagious — and without a lot of effort. That's why marketing is the ideal breeding ground for taking full advantage of the power of memes. If you consider some of the greatest marketing campaigns in history, you'll discover that these three factors were usually fundamental to their success.

The ten most powerful icons of the twentieth century

Let's take a moment to investigate the ten marketing campaigns selected by *Advertising Age* as offering the ten most powerful icons of the twentieth century. Had memes been in vogue when these were selected, perhaps the word *meme* would have been used in place of the word *icon.*

Notice how each of these icons delivers just what memes deliver:

1. The Marlboro Man — Marlboro cigarettes
2. Ronald McDonald — McDonald's restaurants
3. The Jolly Green Giant — Green Giant vegetables
4. Betty Crocker — Betty Crocker food products
5. The Energizer Bunny — Eveready Energizer batteries
6. The Pillsbury Doughboy — assorted Pillsbury foods
7. Aunt Jemima — Aunt Jemima pancake mixes and syrup

8. The Michelin Man — Michelin tires
9. Tony the Tiger — Kellogg's Frosted Flakes
10. Elsie the Cow — Borden dairy products

All but one of these campaigns were around long before Dawkins invented the word *meme*. Each of the memes mentioned earlier represents an entire idea. Memes are always ideas, but ideas are not always memes.

If the ideas are distilled, compressed, simplified, and focused, then presented in a manner that can be communicated through a wide range of media — from the Internet to a billboard — they might become memes.

But not all great ideas, and not even all great marketing campaigns, furnish us with a meme. To see this up close and personal, study the top ten slogans of the past century, again selected by *Advertising Age*. Some have memes. Some do not. Those with memes tell us about the product being marketed. Those without memes tell us nothing about the product or its benefits.

The top ten slogans of the twentieth century

1. "Diamonds are forever" (De Beers) — the three words are a meme
2. "Just do it!" (Nike) — no meme here, just three words
3. "The pause that refreshes" (Coca-Cola) — definitely a meme
4. "Tastes great, less filling" (Miller Lite) — a meme without question

5. "We try harder" (Avis) — a meme telling us about the company

6. "Good to the last drop" (Maxwell House) — a meme about the product

7. "Breakfast of champions" (Wheaties) — another meme about the product

8. "Does she . . . or doesn't she?" (Clairol) — a meme at work

9. "When it rains it pours" (Morton Salt) — a meme with a visual

10. "Where's the beef?" (Wendy's) — a short-lived meme, if a meme at all

Social conscience rarely enters into a person's purchasing behavior. As *Advertising Age* noted, "It will amuse some, and horrify others, that in the pantheon — what we judge to be the ten greatest advertising campaigns ever — are included two air polluters (VW and Avis), nutritionless sugar water (Coca-Cola), one reviled carcinogen (Marlboro), two companies infamous for the use of virtual slave labor (DeBeers, Nike), one purveyor of savory cardiovascular time bombs (McDonald's), two booze peddlers (Absolut and Miller Lite) and one cosmetic product preying on the vanity of women (Clairol)." Fortunately, cause-related marketing is coming to the fore.

To get your meme consciousness into even higher gear, consider the slogans selected for honorable mentions:

"Look, Ma, no cavities!" (Crest toothpaste) — a meme about a product

"Let your fingers do the walking" (Yellow Pages) — a
meme with a visual

"Loose lips sink ships" (public service) — a meme with a
visual

"M&Ms melt in your mouth, not in your hand" (M&M
candies) — a meme

"We bring good things to life" (General Electric) — not
really a meme

Memes-r-us

You can find a lot of memes when you look at the totems used
in centuries past, the tattoos worn by people today, the insig-
nias used by their clubs, and the symbols of the organizations
to which they belong. Many cultures have memes of their own;
for the counterculture of the sixties, tie-dyed garments, long
hair, and flowers served as memes. Pictographs and petro-
glyphs are memes of ancient cultures. Egyptian hieroglyph-
ics were certainly memes, as are the characters in many Orien-
tal languages. When meme-spotting, remember the holidays.
Christmas gives us a long list of memes, from Santa to the
Christmas tree. And who does not connect eggs and bunnies
with Easter?

Nonmarketing memes

Although there are several memes that have been used in marketing, such as Elsie the Cow for Borden's, an arm and a hammer for Arm & Hammer Baking Soda, Camel cigarettes' Joe

Camel, MGM's lion, Paramount's mountain, and Columbia's woman standing with a torch, along with Smokey the Bear for fire prevention and McGruff the Crime Dog for crime prevention, most memes have had little to do with marketing. That's a shame, since memes convey their ideas instantly. For example:

The outstretched thumb of a hitchhiker

The thumbs-up sign for positivity

The middle finger for negativity

Three fingers representing the Boy Scouts of America

The fish for Christianity

Flashing headlights to say, "Your brights are on!"

The dove and the olive branch to signify peace

The blindfolded woman holding scales to indicate justice

The caduceus wand to symbolize medicine

The rainbow to symbolize Hawaii, homosexuality, and the Rainbow Coalition

The anchor to signify a sailor

The flamingo to signify Florida

The eagle standing for the USA

Purple for royalty

A pink triangle for gay and lesbian causes

And one of our newest memes: "Is that your final answer?"

All of this goes to show that memes can take many forms and stand for many causes unrelated to marketing.

Musical memes

Memes can be musical as well as visual or verbal, as proven by these jingles selected by *Advertising Age* as the top ten of the twentieth century:

1. "You deserve a break today" (McDonald's)
2. "Be all that you can be" (U.S. Army)
3. "Pepsi-Cola hits the spot" (Pepsi-Cola)
4. "Mmmm, mmmm, good" (Campbell's)
5. "See the USA in your Chevrolet" (GM)
6. "I wish I was an Oscar Meyer wiener" (Oscar Meyer)
7. "Double your pleasure, double your fun" (Wrigley's Doublemint gum)
8. "Winston tastes good like a cigarette should" (Winston)
9. "It's the real thing" (Coca-Cola)
10. "A little dab'll do ya" (Brylcreem)

All of these jingles led to product success. Some had visual components, such as the Doublemint jingle, but most relied on words and music. Nevertheless, they satisfied the criteria for a meme.

Memes are not merely subversive, manipulative devices dreamed up by ad agencies. In fact, most are by-products of our evolutionary psychology.

If you're wondering how advertising managed to be successful before memes were identified, remember that just as some people have a natural talent for music, art, or mechanics, other people have a natural talent for memes.

Memes as button-pushers

In the marketing context, the most powerful memes of all push emotional hot buttons. The biggest of these buttons are fear, food, and sex. Marketing memes that push any of these three buttons are already primed for success. But those certainly aren't the only buttons. Other buttons activate behaviors based on dreams, greed, scarcity, authority, attraction, success, escape, popularity, pride, achievement, distinction, solutions, curiosity, guilt, maternal and paternal love, romance, family, travel, fashion, thrill, excitement, security, health, youth, fun, and a raftload more. Everybody has hot buttons, emotional and otherwise. The best memes of all are the ultimate button-pushers.

Whatever you do, don't confuse memes with glib statements. Memes transmit specific information. When Avis used its highly successful meme "We're number two, so we try harder," it was actually the number-three car rental company, trailing both Hertz and National. But that meme, dishonest as it was, enabled Avis to leapfrog into the number-two spot. As a guerrilla, you should not distort the truth as Avis did. But you should also know that the meme caused Avis to be viewed in a different light and to be accepted by countless customers. Avis rentals soared, but Avis cars, rental rates, and service didn't change. The meme did all the hard work.

A word to the wise: if you are launching a new company or product, try to come up with a name that is also a meme — as Lean Cuisine did. Brands that do that can save a lot of marketing money because they need not educate the public about what they are. Their names tell the story for them. Alas, such is not true for companies with names like Lucent, Oracle, DHL, Agilent, Cingular, and countless others that spend a fortune telling people something meaningless rather than telling them something meaningful with a simple name that doubles as a meme. ABC is the name of a major network, but it would serve as a fair to middling meme for a company making children's toys.

No place for meaninglessness

Just as commonplace as names that suggest nothing are generic memes that mean nothing. The Jeep Wrangler ran a billboard showing a sport utility vehicle parked on a deserted beach. The copy said, "Park wherever you damn please." Sounds like a meme and acts like a meme, but it isn't really a meme because, on a billboard, the Jeep looks like any other SUV, so the meme ends up representing all four-wheel-drive vehicles rather than the Jeep Wrangler. Such is often the case when marketing people get carried away by cleverness and forget about working to make sure their specific brand has an impact. The people who created that billboard failed to lock in their Wrangler as part of the meme. Instead, it was merely added on. It's true that for many years Jeep was the only four-wheel-drive vehicle for sale, but that was a long, long time ago. Guerrillas are very careful not to live in the past.

Guerrillas create marketing that uses a meme as the centerpiece, the focal point. But keep in mind that you must begin that process with a strategy and then an idea. Your job is to express that idea as simply as possible. Geoff Ayling gives you a memory crutch to help you in that quest. His meme to help you create memes: "When you need a meme, just call in the

TEAM." TEAM stands for "transplant, enhance, adapt, and modify."

Transplant means taking something that isn't quite a meme and turning it into a meme. I was in the meeting at the Leo Burnett advertising agency when we first landed the United Airlines account. The boss asked each member of the creative group to come up with a brief advertisement for United. One member of the group read his innocuous headline, then read his copy. It ended with, "So when you want to fly the friendly skies of United, be sure that you — " and then the boss interrupted. He said, "Read that line again, Tom." Tom read it again, and the boss lit up, saying, "Friendly Skies of United. That's too good to be merely a line of copy. Let's build a campaign around it!" He had transplanted simple words into a meme.

Enhance means taking a simple fact and romancing it. Burger King did that when it used its flame-broiling method of hamburger preparation and centered an entire marketing campaign on it.

Adapt means taking an existing concept and making it your own. Many grocery stores used to have signs saying, "Please don't squeeze the fresh fruit or vegetables." Charmin tissue adapted that idea to focus on the softness of its product. Mr. Whipple caused the brand to soar with the meme "Please don't squeeze the Charmin."

And finally, *modify* means using a set of words known by everyone and modifying them to suit your brand. Everyone knows what "taking a licking" means. But Timex rode to glory when it modified that phrase to describe the ability of its watches to withstand what it termed "torture tests." The Timex meme: "Takes a licking and keeps on ticking."

At the movies

Here's another hint to help you create a meme of your own. Think of movies that use one key frame as the basis of an advertising poster. That key frame serves a meme — a simple image suggesting an entire idea. Look for the key frame in your product or service and determine how you can transform it into a meme.

Don't expect to find marketing memes all over the place. You sure won't find many when you surf the Net, watch the boob tube, or scan your daily newspaper. That is precisely why most advertising is ignored and most advertising investments are wasted. Marketing headlines ought to intrigue or inform, at least planting the seed of a meme. Instead, they usually rhyme or present fluff or a cliché. This makes them incredibly easy to ignore.

The sad truth about your prospects

To illustrate the necessity for a meme, just examine what your prospects are all about. They fit your customer profile. They have spendable funds. They're ready to part with their money. They're willing to make a purchase. And they are precisely the kind of people you'd love to add to your customer list. But — and this is an enormous but — they have no intention of buying from you. They just plain don't need what you're offering, and they're very happy buying from their existing suppliers, some of them your competitors. They're not really hostile toward your company or your offering — just indifferent.

So the big question is: What would have to happen to move

them from being indifferent about your product to being recep-
tive? Here are the two answers:

1. Get inside your prospects' heads and connect with them.
   This is not easy, but I never said creating memes was
   easy. In the previous chapter, I did tell you fifty ways to
   connect with people, and one huge way that is a freeway
   into their heads — showing them how to avoid pain. You
   must make a connection or you'll never make a sale.
   Where to find that connection?

2. View your offering from the standpoint of a prospect.
   When you create a shift in perception, you can create a
   shift in attitude, which can create a shift in behavior —
   and that's the goal of all marketing.

Once you have made a connection with your prospect, communicate something that moves that person from a state of indifference to a state of desiring what you offer. You see a wristwatch that is rather ho-hum, but then you see the watch being
fastened to the propeller blade of a speedboat, which takes off
in a roar. Your attitude shifts from indifference to fascination.
At the end of the boat ride, the watch is removed from the blade
and seen to be still ticking. Your attitude shifts again into one
of desiring such a durable watch. The visual meme is the "torture test." The verbal meme: "Takes a licking and keeps on
ticking." This powerful meme put Timex watches on the map,
not to mention on millions of wrists.

These two answers point you in the right direction. But they
don't take you to that promised land where prospects are con-
verted to customers. That requires more work on your part.

Never forget that your prospects are besieged with marketing every single day, so much so that they don't even resent it — they just ignore it. It's far easier to ignore something than to resent it. After all, when a person resents something, at least some emotion is involved. When they ignore it, there is no emotion.

Your biggest barrier

Your biggest barrier to implanting your meme in the minds of your prospects is the proliferation of marketing. Your enemy is not necessarily the competition. It's sensory overload. Memes break through that overload. Guerrilla creativity surmounts it every time.

Guerrilla creativity even surmounts the accountant mentality that directs most companies. This mentality focuses only on the bottom line, demands instant results, doesn't understand the real cost of acquiring a new customer through marketing, and fails to factor in the lifetime value of a customer.

That mentality is the reason why brands spend a fortune educating prospects about the company name and not investing much in telling them what that name stands for or how it can improve their lives. It's the mentality that causes people to think their audience wants to know about their company. It is responsible for marketing aimed at the head and not at the heart. The reality is that marketing doesn't have as much to do with fact as with perception.

Because many people in marketing tend to fall head over heels in love with their own creativity, I'm waving a red flag of danger to them with one hand, and with the other I'm waving a flag that says, "Direct your attention to creating memes in your marketing!" To stimulate your meme-ory, let's examine some of the world's most successful memes.

Some of history's most successful memes

Besides having a thorough knowledge of your offering and your audience, you'll be helped immensely if you are aware of other memes that have withstood the test of time and do their job with aplomb. Although many of those memes were not used for marketing, all of them contain a lesson for would-be meme-meisters.

1. The Jolly Green Giant is a meme that conveys the idea of veggies in a healthful setting, overlooked by a large, effective, and happy giant who is even able to serve as the company spokesman, though he never says anything besides "Ho-ho-ho."

2. The cross is a very powerful meme that suggests God. For centuries it has served as a centerpiece meme in cities and towns throughout the world. One glance at it and people know the message.

3. Ronald McDonald is a meme that suggests kids, goodness, fun, and good deeds. Obviously, McDonald's wants this favorable association to carry over to its franchises. It does, to the company's delight.

4. The Marlboro Man meme suggests masculinity, freedom, adventure, and individuality. He personally elevated Marlboro's ranking from thirty-first in America to first in the world . . . without ever uttering a word. To keep him pristine, none of the ads in which he appears

ever feature a woman or cattle . . . just guys with rugged good looks and horses.

5. The meme expressed by the logo carrying the words "Intel inside" conveys confidence that the computer is up to date, highly effective, powerful, and reliable.

6. The Doublemint meme communicated "double the pleasure and double the fun" while implanting the name of the gum. People only had to see the two women cavorting in the sunshine and immediately were able to identify the gum and its attributes.

7. M&Ms show the meme of people holding the candy, then putting it in their mouths, then holding out their hands to show that they're clean, all neatly tied up with the theme line of "melts in your mouth, not in your hands."

8. NBC used a peacock as a meme to convey the idea that it telecast in full color, and although every station now telecasts in full color, NBC has retained its meme to identify the station as a leader.

9. Dreyfus Funds used a lion as its meme to show the power and permanence of Dreyfus. Just seeing that lion walking on Wall Street was enough to suggest both Dreyfus and power to people.

10. The Michelin Man is a meme whose roly-poly body suggests comfort, as well as friendliness. Everyone who sees him immediately thinks of Michelin and associates it with comfort and safety.

11. The word *guerrilla* is a meme that shows people how to attain conventional goals using unconventional means. The camouflage design on the cover implants the idea of guerrilla even deeper. Just think — Houghton Mifflin has its very own meme, and you're holding it in your hands!

Nonmarketing memes

The swastika, although an archetypical symbol from centuries past, used by ancient cultures to represent peace, is now a meme for evil.

The Star of David has become a meme for Judaism. One glance at it and you know what it represents.

A flag is a meme representing a nation and its people. In fact, flags are among the most popular memes on earth.

The words "Don't tread on me," combined with a symbol of a snake, became a powerful meme signifying independence. Small wonder it was used on a flag.

The Red Cross is a meme that signifies both humanity and the present moment. It crosses all cultural lines and carries meaning for virtually all people on earth.

The skull-and-crossbones was a meme for pirates and now is a meme for poison. No words are needed. The visual symbols are eloquent enough.

Among the newest memes in the world are international traffic signs, which must convey their message instantly and clearly. When you see a sign with a diagonal line through a symbol, you know you're being warned about a no-no.

The disabled symbol of a person in a wheelchair is identified worldwide yet is the essence of simplicity. No words are needed.

Recently, a ribbon has become a meme for the search for a cure.

The heart has long been a meme for love and romance.

A man in a white coat is a simple and widespread meme for a doctor.

Bars across America feature a sign with a martini glass as a cocktail meme.

Everyone knows that a lightbulb above a person's head is a meme representing a good idea.

The snail is a recognizable meme for slowness.

The globe is a meme representing the world — and most of the world knows exactly what it means.

Some memes are unintentional, such as a smoldering fire, a meme that means someone was recently in the vicinity. The same holds for animal tracks, which indicate that some critter has passed that way.

How long have the four-leaf clover and the leprechaun been memes representing Ireland?

And let's not forget memes that have been successfully used in marketing: Mickey Mouse is a meme that is so self-explanatory that I won't waste your time explaining it.

A newer meme is the practice of winning teams pouring

Gatorade on their coach. No words. But when you see that liquid poured on a deliriously happy coach, you can't help but associate Gatorade with winning.

A radar for memes

A good exercise for guerrillas who wish to develop a meme for their companies is to develop a radar for existing memes. Surf the Net, scan a magazine, and view commercials with an eye toward spotting memes. Once you find one, think backward from the meme to the original idea; try to follow the thought process that generated the meme. When you see an illustration of an elderly man with a small beard and a big smile, you immediately recognize him as Colonel Sanders. How do you suppose the company came up with that meme? It's pretty easy to tell, just by considering the name of the company and the guy who mixed all those herbs and spices to create his chicken recipe. No heavy thinking necessary.

But don't lose sight of the fact that memes were here way before the Colonel. Memes are expressions of ideas — usually complex ideas that form themselves into distinct, memorable units — such as these common and ancient memes:

Arches
Wearing clothes
Alphabets
Calendars
Calculus
Chess

Perspective drawings

Impressionism

Evolution and memes

Those examples prove that the evolution of memes could not get started until evolution had paved the way by creating a species — *Homo sapiens* — with brains that could provide shelter, and habits of communication that could provide transmission conduits for memes. Those conduits are now called the media.

The hallmark of guerrilla creativity

A powerful meme is the hallmark of guerrilla creativity. It implants an idea in the minds of your prospects. And it reduces the cost of your marketing because you don't have to spend so much on educating people. So when you come up with a meme for your own company, learn to cherish it and dismiss all thoughts of abandoning it.

To paraphrase the United Negro College Fund's meme, "A mind is a terrible thing to waste," I remind you that a meme is also a terrible thing to waste.

4

Where Creativity Is Born

▶ ▶ ▶ *Simple Research Can Result*
in Invaluable Knowledge

THE MORE YOU KNOW, the more creative you can be.
If you want to create a meme for your company, you've
got to know a whale of a lot about your offering and
about your audience. Your offering and your audience are the
mother lodes you must mine in order to come up with a meme
worth far more than its weight in gold.

Start by looking at your offering. Most people get the majority of their information visually. So it will help you to think of
your company in a visual sense. If you offer a product or service that saves time, how might you visualize that? A clock? A
watch? A calendar? All three denote time, and all three should
be considered if you want to create a time-based meme. Do you
have an offering that helps people attract members of the opposite sex? You can express that visually by showing a happy
couple, a heart, a kiss. All three are the basis for memes that
look like your promise.

Although I hope that you'll create both a visual and a verbal meme, I know that you'll succeed faster if you always remember that memes are ideas first, and expressions of those ideas second.

In the *New York Times,* back in 1996, Edward Rothstein penned an on-the-button column about memes:

> This column may infect you.
>
> This is not something you will be aware of at first. The words will just pass by, inspiring impatience or curiosity. But by the end there will be no turning back. You will be infected with a meme.
>
> And it is catching. Which is the whole point. A meme is like a virus, except it works on minds rather than bodies. Memes (rhymes with "schemes") are ideas that alter the ways in which we think. They hold on and don't let go unless displaced by rival memes. They can lead to phenomena as trivial as Hula-Hoops or as substantial as Christianity.
>
> Their effects can be seen in backward-turned baseball hats and in philosophical treatises, in religious cults and in ideological manifestoes. And they can be felt in the power of songs or jingles, which seem to take on lives of their own, propagating, varying, repeating, demanding attention.

Requirements of a meme

That column captures the essence of memes, and its message should be taken to heart when you go about creating your own meme. Some of the requirements of that meme will be:

- It takes just a few seconds for readers, viewers, or listeners to get the point of your idea.
- It is worthwhile for some customers to redistribute the meme.
- Your meme is extendable and mutates easily.

The technology to communicate your meme should be as trivial as possible.

Because we're living in a global society more than ever, your meme will be more powerful if it can cross all cultural and linguistic lines.

Bad news for accountants

Memes express ideas instantly but don't necessarily work their miracles instantly. This comes as terrible news to those of the accountant mentality who demand immediate results. But it comes as no news to guerrillas, who have long since learned the rewards of patience.

The point for you is that speed is not of the essence, and neither is originality. We're talking profits and longevity here, certainty and clarity. If it worked five thousand years ago, there's a very good chance it will work today, because people have not really changed very much since the days of Uba the caveman.

Sometimes a company develops a meme, thinks it's a great meme, then runs with it — only to find that it did not have much longevity. Such was the case with Taco Bell's famed chihuahua. Although it was widely recognized and liked by consumers, sagging sales prompted its elimination.

Staying power

The moral is a lesson for guerrillas: it's unwise to create a widely recognizable meme without staying power. The trick is to create a meme that does not become old and worn out. As you've seen, many memes live thousands of years, gaining strength with time rather than growing old and useless.

In the back of your mind, always remember that great marketing has very little to do with selling and everything to do with buying. Remember also that most marketing falls on its face: people don't respond to it because they've forgotten it by the time they're ready to make a purchase.

The starting point for a meme

The starting point for a meme already exists. It's in your product or service. Remove all traces of modesty and then create a list of your offering's benefits. Make this a long list. As you consider each benefit, think of a graphic symbol of that benefit. Think of a brief set of words, or perhaps a single word that summarizes the benefit. If you try hard enough, you'll discover that every one of your benefits can be translated visually. That means you'll end up with a selection of meme possibilities.

Before settling on any one of them, make another list, this time a list of characteristics describing your customers. Once again, each characteristic can be represented by a symbol. If customers are interested in security, a fence might represent that. A focus on improving profits could be expressed visually by a dollar sign or a growth curve. The more you understand what makes your customers tick, the better equipped you'll be to create a meme that appeals to people just like your customers.

Besides researching your own offering and your audience, you'll also gain by seriously researching your marketplace, your competition, the media you'll be using, your industry, and successful advertising of the past. Whatever you do, don't think in terms of originality as much as profitability for your company.

When it comes to marketing, guerrillas become creative in very special ways, and they're not the ways demonstrated by most marketing.

What color is your meme?

Guerrilla creativity moves into an even higher gear when you become aware of the deep, nonverbal meaning of colors. Although your meme may be viewed in black and white in newspapers and yellow and black in the yellow pages, the colors you use in the meme can say something very eloquent about your business.

Elegant colors include gold, silver, chocolate, maroon, and navy blue. Some of the fresh, healthy colors are yellow, bright blue, and green. Red, yellow, blue, orange, and purple are loud and aggressive colors, though purple also denotes spirituality. Brown, tan, burnt orange, subdued greens, and earth tones are among the natural colors. Keep these findings in mind when creating your meme. You want the colors you choose for your meme to reflect your overall identity.

While the use of color is an extra expense with print materials, it is free on the Internet. That's why you see so many colors on Web sites. But keep in mind that, unlike printed colors, which you see as light reflected off the ink on a page, Web-site colors are projected from your computer monitor directly into a visitor's eyes. Overuse of bright colors in the Internet environment can easily strain the eyes and the patience of your visitors. Brightly colored backgrounds are also likely to make the reading of text very difficult — difficult enough that I find myself clicking away from the site rather than risk eyestrain.

The job of the guerrilla is to employ background colors that are pleasing to the eye, yet not so bright as to detract from your headlines and text, and certainly not from your meme. Make sure the color you use for your text is extremely easy to read against a colored background. Maroon text may be handsome, but viewed against a purple background, it becomes infuriating.

The colors you select for your meme should be consistent so that they become your signature colors. Don't forget — it's not the Valley of the Jolly Green, Lavender, and Puce Giant.

How guerrillas view creativity

Guerrillas view creativity in marketing the same way drivers view steering wheels in their cars. Creativity is supposed to guide the marketing toward its goal of producing profits just as the steering wheel is supposed to guide the car toward its goal of arriving safely at the destination.

It doesn't always work out that way. Just as there are tragedies on the highway because accidents happen, there are tragedies in marketing, and none of them have to happen. Worse yet, they don't even happen by accident. People actually plan, sweat over, and focus hard on marketing that is headed from the start directly toward disaster.

Ten insights into marketing creativity

Guerrillas view marketing with ten insights into marketing creativity that illuminate the path for them. These insights prevent them from going over the edge, losing their way, or wasting their time and money. Why wait? Here are the ten insights —

each one to be applied when you're considering how you'll create a meme for your business:

1. *Creativity in marketing should be measured solely by how well it contributes to your overall profitability.* If it helps you sell at profit, it is creative, and if it doesn't, it's not creative. That makes creativity easy to measure. Awards and compliments have nothing to do with creative marketing.

2. *Creativity should always be measured by its ability to withstand repetition,* because purchase decisions are made with the unconscious mind and repetition is the best way to access the unconscious. If your creative marketing idea and meme can get stronger with repetition, you've got a winner.

3. *Using humor in your creative marketing efforts is like reaching into a bag filled with poisonous snakes.* Not only might you get hurt on your very first reach into the bag, but the more you reach the more it works against you, because repetition helps marketing but murders humor.

4. *Any creativity in marketing that is not directed toward motivating a purchase is like employing a vampire in your marketing.* The vampire sucks attention away from your prime offer, your benefits, and your main idea in an inane attempt to be creative at the expense of your profitability.

5. *Creativity should be seen as an opportunity not for show business but for sell business.* Marketing is business far more than entertainment, and although it may be en-

tertaining, that is not its prime requirement. It exists mainly to create a desire to buy, not mainly to entertain.

6. *Creativity is a way to not merely mention your name but to implant it and connect it with something positive.* Gain awareness and a crucial position in the minds of your prospects by showing and saying your name creatively, helping people remember your name the next time they're in the market for what you sell. But remembering your name is not enough all by itself. The key is to get people to remember your name and the reasons they should purchase what you are marketing. A powerful meme accomplishes that.

7. *Creativity in marketing is meeting the challenge of demonstrating your benefit in a way that people will remember.* It is important that your prospects remember your name, and equally important that they learn what makes you special and why they should own what you are offering. It's not too difficult to do that with a lot of text and pictures. But it's a different story when you're creating a meme and must use graphic shorthand to convey your point.

8. *Creativity comes not from inspiration, or even perspiration, but from knowledge.* The more knowledge you have, the more creative you can be. You need to know your benefits, prospects, industry, competition, media options, and the Internet — for starters.

9. *Creativity begins not with a headline, graphic idea, special effect, or jingle, but with an idea.* The idea should center on your offer, your competitive advantage, or

your main benefit — and it should come singing clearly through your marketing in any medium.

10. *Creativity of the highest form in marketing has longevity and improves with age.* How long has a diamond been forever? How long have United's skies been friendly? How long has the Maytag repairman been lonely? Great marketing creativity is both flexible and enduring.

It's a cinch to sit here in my comfy chair typing out a bunch of insights about how you should be creative. It's easy for me and hard for you. But hey, I've got my job and you've got yours. I'd like to tell you that it's going to be simple and that the list of businesses with timeless marketing creativity goes on and on.

But I'd be lying, because it's a short list. Amazingly short. Most business owners have this ridiculous notion that their marketing is supposed to change constantly. And most people who create marketing have their eyes on their awards wall, not on your bottom line.

So it's going to be a tough job for you to separate true creativity from pretend creativity. Most marketing you see these days is of the pretend variety. Still, armed with these insights, the creativity you employ will be guerrilla creativity, and it will lead you not down the garden path but directly to your bank vault.

The importance of passion

Along with insights, you must have passion for these five things:

1. *Your product or service:* That passion will stoke your creative fires.

2. *Your customers and prospects:* You know your offering can improve their lives, and you want like crazy to do that because you sincerely care about these good people. Do you care more about them than your bottom line? The answer is that you'd better or your crassness will become apparent.

3. *Clarity in communications:* Many people creating marketing have a lot of important things to convey to you, but verbiage obfuscates their message. Your goal must be absolute clarity, which is a function of a winning meme.

4. *Marketing:* Rather than being embarrassed that you are marketing, you are excited at the opportunity to turn the world, or at least your target market, on to the glorious things that you offer. You do not try to hide the fact that it is marketing, but you do make an attempt to communicate your message loud and clear — with passion for both your product and your opportunity to spread the word about it.

5. *Memes:* As you wrap your mind around the power of memes and then create one for your own business, you'll be passing your competitors in a newly created fast lane. By the time they even understand the notion of memes, yours will be implanted in the minds of your customers and prospects and you will own your niche.

You may already feel passionate about four of these five things, but I doubt that you're passionate yet about memes. I suspect that the more you learn about them and experiment with creating them, then use them, the more a fire will begin to burn within you — a passion for having your very own meme. Memes have been with us for a long time, they're here to stay, and they're only going to become more prevalent in the future.

If you own a business, one of these days you're going to want a meme, to create a meme and discover how it energizes your marketing. The sooner that day comes, the more powerful your meme will be — because the recognition factor of memes strengthens with time.

By calling your attention to memes in these pages, I'm trying to create the momentum in your mind to create your own meme, put it before your public, then ride it all the way to the bank.

5

A Technique for Being Creative

▶ ▶ ▶ *Transforming Yourself into*
   a Creative Genius

Y ES, YOU ARE CREATIVE. No, it doesn't matter if
you haven't written or painted anything of note up until
now because even with zero creative experience in the
past, every living human is capable of generating truly creative
ideas. The knack you need is the knack of knowing the difference between substance and style.

Because we're smack dab in the middle of the Information Age, and because time is so darned important, guerrillas
do not waste the time of their prospects and customers with
gimmicks and pizzazz. Instead, guerrillas reward their time
with beneficial information and solid content. The substance of
guerrilla marketing is so lush yet concise that *substance is their
style.*

Is your current marketing distinctive because of its style or
its substance? The ideal answer is *both*. With its style, your
marketing conveys your identity and captures the attention of
your targeted audience. With its substance, it gives essential
facts and motivates that audience.

Well-informed marketers see to it that both their style and their substance are obvious but that their product or service always has the starring role in their marketing.

We've all had the experience of viewing a TV spot or reading an ad and wondering what the heck it's about, so you know what I'm getting at. It's even worse online; many Web sites are more confusing than enlightening.

It floats

In the early days of marketing, nobody needed special effects to be creative. When Harley Procter and his cousin, James Gamble, churned their soap too long and it floated, they proclaimed Ivory the soap that floats — a meme that instantly set it apart from its competition. Later they declared it was 99 and 44/100ths percent pure. People knew exactly what they meant. That number was also their meme.

But now the creative revolution is upon us. In the name of *creativity* rather than the less glamorous but more accurate name of *selling,* billions of dollars are being wasted each year. And that's a conservative estimate.

The creative rebels, award winners almost every one of them, are carried away by style, and in the melee, substance gets lost. Marketing is definitely not a shuck and jive show or an entertainment medium. Its purpose is selling, and it should therefore be loaded with substance.

Tap dancing and cartwheeling

You can be sure that the top salespeople in the world don't begin their presentations with a tap dance or a cartwheel. They succeed because of the substance they provide with a certain style, not because of the style itself.

The overriding concept in your marketing should be *to present substance and do it with style.* The emphasis is on the substance. Readers, viewers, and Web site visitors remember the substance. Checks are written, credit cards used, and orders placed because of the substance.

Be on guard against the multitude of "creative" people who populate the marketing profession. Too many of them have been trained to create a gorgeous picture, a rhyming headline, or a flashing Web site when they should be trying to create an eye-popping upswing in your sales curve.

That sales curve is your responsibility. Remember that if "creative" ideas cost you more than they earn for you, something is wrong with the equation. Guerrillas know that the equation should read: "creativity equals profits."

Substance versus style

Substance consists of both facts and opinions. It communicates both features and benefits. It is as specific as it can possibly be, as specific as 99 and 44/100ths percent pure. And it effectively utilizes both words and pictures. What substance isn't is *fun* — and you shouldn't try to make people think that it is unless you sell video games or bicycles.

It's *style* that's fun. Style makes marketing enjoyable to read and hear. Or at least it makes marketing digestible. Remember that your competition isn't Hollywood. It's that company that's been selling to your customers and attracting your prospects. Your competitors are people who don't have stars in their eyes, simply profits on their mind.

Given the relationship of substance to style, put your money on substance every time. But be aware that there are exceptions to this rule. If, for example, the very essence of your product or service is its style, you may want to convey that style as its primary benefit. The style is its substance.

But most businesses should *not even think* of selling with style at the expense of substance. Many have tried. Most have failed. Your task: stress your substance, and do it with style.

Marketing as a mating ritual

Before showing you a time-honored and simple technique for coming up with creative ideas, I think it's important for you to view the creative process in a new way, a way that can add a sense of reality to your expectations and a great deal of effectiveness to your marketing. *Look at marketing as a mating ritual.* Your prospects are those with whom you want to mate.

The whole idea of guerrilla marketing is to transform cold prospects into consenting partners. As with superb sex, marketers shouldn't be in a hurry, nor should they direct their energies toward disinterested people. You must remember that a loving relationship isn't consummated without proper wooing and knowing exactly what turns on the prospect. Learning what turns them on should be one of the goals of your research. The more you know about your prospect's hot buttons, the more targeted your meme can be.

When small-business owners think of marketing not so much as impersonal communication as sexual journey, they are far more successful in their marketing. In today's cluttered marketing environment, instead of pondering numbers and demographics, explore the concepts of romance and love. That means realizing that falling in love with the right person and keeping the relationship delicious and satisfying is not so much a single major event as a step-by-step process.

It begins by *playing the field* and determining just whom you want to date in the first place. In this step, guerrilla marketers concentrate on the compatibility factor. They set their radar to find prospects with whom the proper chemistry will lead to mutual understanding and eventual consent. Unfazed by superficial allure, they seek soulmates more than customers. Their taste and discretion help reduce their marketing costs because their targets reflect quality over quantity.

The guerrilla marketer's next step is *gaining knowledge of your beloved.* He seeks information about prospects who have caught his fancy so he can satisfy their needs more than their wants — because the guerrilla realizes that people often want what they don't need, and providing it is hardly the basis of a long-term relationship. The guerrilla seeks shared values in customers, much as two people with romance on their minds do in getting to know each other. After learning the ways of their prospects through research and two-way communication, the guerrilla then treats all prospects differently, just as each one wants to be treated.

At this point, the guerrilla engages in *flirting* — taking that first step toward gaining consent. Marketing with personalized messages, treating advertising not as the way to make the sale but as the first step in gaining consent, the guerrilla works on making the offering attractive to those prospects who have attracted him.

When *the courtship* begins, the guerrilla pays very close attention and proves that he cares. He enters into dialogues with those after whom he is lusting, and he knows what to say so that his lust will be returned. Any courtship is intensified with gifts of love, and it is no different in the guerrilla marketer's search for consenting partners. Gifts can be gift-wrapped or offered in the form of prizes, memberships in loyalty groups, newsletters, booklets, or regular e-mail updates. Each prospect knows that his or her individuality is recognized.

Next comes *making out,* connecting even more closely with prospects by becoming more intimate in marketing. Perhaps the guerrilla sends valuable information, possibly a questionnaire, maybe even an invitation to a special event. By listening carefully to the prospects' likes, dislikes, and specific problems, guerrillas learn to make promises they can keep. Their penchant for taking action makes the consent for which they strive even broader.

The step in marketing that most relates to *foreplay* is when marketers give to their partners the exact pleasure that they want. They capitalize on the interactivity afforded by online communications to become a part of their prospect's identity. They customize their messages to each prospect, not only making them feel special but proving their devotion. Foreplay need not be confined to online communications. It works just as well offline when guerrillas invite and continue dialogue by mail, on the phone, and even in person. The Internet makes interactivity a lot easier, but the idea of it has been with us a lot longer than computers.

Guerrilla marketers and their prospects achieve *consummation* by closing the sale with mutual consent. Rather than having rushed, their timing is impeccable and their fulfillment implies a commitment. The marketer has consistently demonstrated empathy for the partner — with the goal of providing joy and satisfaction. The earth may not tremble, but a lasting bond has been created.

During *the afterglow,* the connection is solidified. This is accomplished with assiduous follow-up that proves, in a manner of speaking, that the marketer still respects the prospect in the morning. When the marketer expresses warm appreciation, such as through a thank-you note or a membership card in a frequent buyers' club, the prospects are so delighted that they cannot help but relate their joy to other people they know.

The marketing process aspires to more than a dalliance; it should lead to the start of *a long and happy marriage.* Your devotion is unmistakable because it has been built on the details you have learned — the specific tastes of each customer and your shared experience of sale, purchase, and use.

The more you view the marketing process as a mating ritual rather than an economic ritual, the longer will be your list of consenting and delighted partners.

Five steps to creativity

There is a process you can use to generate your own creative ideas to come up with a meme that will woo and win your prospects, represent your company in all the media, look as great in the yellow pages as it does on a Web site, and come across as powerfully on stationery as it does in a television commercial. It's a very simple process, one that will prove to you beyond doubt that you're a highly creative individual. One of the most winning aspects of this process is how brief it is. It has only five steps.

Start the process by investing fifteen minutes of your precious time trying to come up with a meme right off the bat. Trust your instincts and pretend you are a highly paid creative director at a big-time advertising agency. Put into writing anything and everything that comes to mind. If you do this, you'll turn off that built-in censor in your mind — the one that says, "Naw, this isn't good enough," the one that scoffs, "This is pure garbage and should never see the light of day," the one that scolds you, "That meme is so bad that it ought to be revised before it's even tossed into the wastebasket."

Everybody has this censor, and almost everybody listens to it. Guerrillas know how to bypass it. They do that by putting all their ideas onto paper, knowing that when the censor is bypassed, when all the ideas are noted, the best ones will come eventually, if not at the start. By putting that edit-crazy part of their mind into a subordinate position, they increase their production of ideas. They think in quantity rather than quality. Quality will come in its own good time. Guerrillas know that they've got to go through a lot of awful stuff before they come up with something halfway decent.

The key here is not to try too hard. When the author and coach Robert Kriegel was training sprinters for the Olympic trials and found them to be tense and tight, he asked them to ease up on their next sprint and go only nine-tenths of their normal intensity. The result was that each runner's time improved, and one actually set an unofficial world's record.

Guerrillas know that during this first step they should *try easy, not hard.* Fifteen minutes of trying easy . . . that's the first step. It's called "direct thinking" because you are trying to come up with a winner directly, right at the start. A very very few people manage to come up with a winning idea or meme at this step. But most continue through the other steps to ensure that they've got exactly what they need.

The second step, which also takes only a quick fifteen minutes, is called "lateral thinking." Spend this time studying the visual representations of the benefits provided by your offering. Think deeply about each benefit and try to determine how you'd express it visually — or even with a set of words, à la Lean Cuisine. During these fifteen minutes, also think about the needs and wants of your target audience. Take into consideration their personal characteristics, and again, try to view your audience's desires in a visual way. The more you can visualize their dreams, the more primed your mind will be when it comes to developing a meme.

It's crucial that you focus intensively during these fifteen minutes. Consider also your competitive advantages, what most differentiates you from your competitors. Concentrate with all your power during this stage to consider all the factors peripheral to the meme you'll create. This is where all your research pays off: since knowledge is the birthplace of creativity, that knowledge will spur your mind to be far more creative than you may have imagined it to be.

To get some perspective on how hard you have to think, consider the words of Rodin, whose sculpture "The Thinker" is one of the most famous ever created. He said, "What makes my Thinker think is that he thinks not only with the brain, with his knitted brow, his distended nostrils and compressed lips, but with every muscle of his arms, back and legs, with his clenched fist and gripping toes." That's how hard you'll have to think, but your hard thinking may be rewarded with a winning meme.

The third step allows you to relax. You focused easily during the first step, then focused hard, concentrating with all your might, during that second step. What you were doing in those steps was priming your unconscious mind. That is the part that makes up 90 percent of your entire mind, and it's an exceptional environment for creativity. Now, during this third step, *take your mind off your goal of creating a meme.* Forget about it. Completely remove it from your consciousness and think about anything you want, except for your new meme. Do anything you want, but don't try to develop your idea. That is happening in your inner, deeper mind and doesn't require any more help from your conscious mind. In fact, if you don't turn the matter over to your unconscious mind and try to create your meme with conscious thought only, you actually impede your unconscious mind as it tries to do its job.

Here's where your unconscious does all the work. It filters through your ideas from the first two steps, your direct and lateral thinking, and serves as a super-fertile ground for growing the fruits of that thinking. During this step, the exact meme you want and need will spring into your mind. It may happen while you're having dinner, taking a shower, watching television, reading, or talking with friends about something entirely different. It may come to you while you're seated on the john reading, telling a story to your kids, or conversing with your life partner. It often comes into your mind as you're falling asleep. In fact, it is not uncommon for the idea to make its way into your consciousness while you are sleeping! Does that mean you should keep a notepad next to your bed? It does not. The idea your mind develops will be so clear, so powerful, and so obvious that you won't forget it — even if you go back to sleep again. You can count on waking up with the same idea in your mind.

Just think — all it takes is for you to let go with your conscious mind and let your unconscious mind kick around and strut its creative stuff. It seems funny that you're at your most creative when you're not trying to be creative. But that's the power of your unconscious mind. It's far more creative than you could ever dream. In this step, your mind knows very well to concentrate on quality and forget quantity. One great idea is all you need. One powerful meme can be the making of your company.

Take the result of the process — the meme for which you have been striving — and measure it against your marketing strategy. Show it to friends, to associates, to people who are aware of your marketing strategy. Invite them to poke holes in it, if indeed holes exist. This is where your creativity is exposed to the bright light of reality.

I'm urging you to show the end result of your creative thinking to others, but don't expect their faces to light up and say, "That's it!" Instead, expect frowns, and then perhaps suggestions for changing your meme. When that happens, remember that there is no marketing strategy so brilliant that it cannot be made utterly ineffective through compromise. And few great ideas — or memes — are recognized as great right from the get-go. You've put a lot of time and effort into coming up with your meme. So worry not; your unconscious mind is up to the task of either convincing your compadres or being a flexible guerrilla. This is where your ego and your steadfastness will be put to the test. And so will your meme.

You can easily test your meme with your prospects rather than your associates — because prospects count for a lot more than buddies when it comes to measuring a meme. Talk about it or show it to as many prospects as you want, but do it one at a time, because that's how they'll view or hear your meme. *Listen to the questions they ask!* If they ask questions about your meme or its meaning, that's a signal that it is not a good meme. If they ask questions about how they can learn more about what you have to offer, your meme is off to a great start and may even be a keeper. Nowhere is it written that you have to slave and struggle to come up with a winner. Memes that invite dialogue are invaluable because dialogue is another road that can lead to a lasting relationship.

This process might take fewer than twenty-four hours and will rarely take more than three days. Don't think this can happen with only four of the five steps. You need all five — or else you'll be operating like a hand without a thumb.

I know that when you employ this technique for your own meme, you'll factor in the realities of communications versus design, customers versus yourself, benefits versus features, and clarity versus uniqueness. You'll come up with an idea that provides you with a meme that works in all the media and is directed right to the inside of your prospects' minds. From your mind to the prospect's mind — that's the right direction.

Stress and creativity

Roy H. Williams, who has earned his appellation as "the Wizard of Ads," claims that the moment of emotional recovery is the best possible time to think about problems you have not been able to solve. To quote the wizard: "Moments of great, creative insight always follow the times of greatest stress. It's a law of the universe."

Here's how Roy explains it:

Think of creativity as an inert gas, a substance unique. An inert gas cannot enter into compounds with other substances because, in each of its atoms, the outer ring of electrons is completely full. An inert gas is completely stable and cannot be changed. Unless you jolt it with too much stimulation.

Pass a current through an inert gas and a single electron in the outer ring of each atom will be pushed into an orbit where it does not belong. But it cannot stay there. As the electron falls back into its proper place, the excess energy will be released as light. This is a miracle witnessed nightly on ten million street corners in America. Without argon and mercury vapor streetlights, America would be a very dark place, indeed. Without the radiant beauty of neon, we would be a much less colorful people.

Recovery from overstimulation is a magical moment. As each crisis dissipates and your emotional electrons return to their proper orbits, don't close your eyes to the light.

This certainly does not mean that I recommend stress, but I do wish to point out that stress has an upside to balance its downside. In that upside, your meme may be waiting.

Always keep in mind that your goal is to motivate a purchase, create a desire, push a hot button, and alter human behavior. Getting laughs is not your goal. Alka-Seltzer's "I can't believe I ate the whole thing!" generated loads of laughs, but with each one, Pepto-Bismol's sales rose because prospects were thinking, "Alka-Seltzer thinks my tummy ache is a big joke and doesn't take my symptoms seriously. I feel terrible, and all I want is something serious to make me feel better."

Being remembered

Being remembered is also not the whole job of a marketing message. Part of the job, yes. The entire job, no. The lying salesman for Isuzu, Joe Isuzu, was the star of the most memorable of all TV commercials for two years running, but during those years Isuzu sales sagged downward at a steady pace. Joe was a failure for Isuzu, and his memorability went for zilch, but he's back again, and this time perhaps he'll be used more effectively. Although having a memorable message is not the entire name of the marketing game, it certainly doesn't hurt your marketing. The key to guerrillas is *what* people remember. People might remember your naked marching band, but they won't remember why they should visit your bookstore.

The famous posters of Uncle Sam pointing at the viewer and saying, "I want *you* for the U.S. Army," were not humorous, nor were they designed to be memorable so much as motivating, but they worked to accomplish their purpose, and with astonishing simplicity — in both World War I and World War II. Memorability would not have helped us win the wars. Motivation had to be the underlying strategy. Incidentally, "Uncle Sam" was really a self-portrait of James Montgomery Flagg, the illustrator. And he did his illustrated poster for free.

The chemistry of creative people

But even for free, a meme is only as good as the marketing strategy that goes with it. And a guerrilla must be at the helm of that strategy. The advertising expert Edward Buxton said:

> Creative people are vain. According to psychologists and other people who studied them, the general view is that creative people have a stronger, more pronounced sense of self. Call it ego, pride of authorship, a larger-than-normal need for praise and approval. In any case, successful creative people do indeed seem to have a need — often bordering on compulsion — to "express them-

selves" — and to the largest and most appreciative audience possible. So be it — it is an integral part of their equipment. It can fuel a burning ambition — or cause untold misery. It usually does both.

So a guerrilla, unburdened by creative baggage, must be on hand to guide the creative geniuses. The guerrilla's job is not to dictate to the creative person, but to ascertain that the creativity is aimed in the proper direction. Today creativity is more important than ever. That's because products these days are all so nearly alike. Those who create marketing for the products must always be asking: What point do I wish to make? Who is my target audience? What do they need? What do I want my viewer to do? Buy now? Simply love my product until he's ready to buy? Move his money from the bank and into an on-line investing account? Feel benevolent about the company for which I'm creating marketing?

The ad great Shirley Polykoff said, "Creativity has always been just a knack or talent for expressing a single idea or simple concept in a fresh arresting new way, then saying it with flair."

The built-in BS detector

While you're expressing it with flair, be certain that you also say it believably, because when it comes to marketing, the public has a built-in BS detector. People take most marketing with a grain of salt, expecting exaggeration and puffery. Of course, your message must be truthful and honest. But getting people to *believe* you're being up-front and open is a formidable task.

Just pretend there is a skeptic standing behind your left shoulder, looking at each word you write, viewing each graphic you suggest, and saying, "I don't believe that for a second!" Calm that skeptic with what the ad great Leo Burnett termed "shirtsleeve English" — clear and simple words, with graphics that are arresting, captivating, and believable. "Automobiles on the highway" isn't as shirtsleeve English as "cars on the road." Shirtsleeve English uses the words people say more than the words they read.

People are natural-born doubters. Descartes didn't say only, "I think, therefore I am." He said, "I doubt, therefore I think. I think, therefore I am." Create your meme to remove all traces of doubt, because that's a barrier you're sure to face.

Some business owners know well that they can't fool all the people all the time, but they make a nice income fooling some of the people some of the time. Today it's getting harder to fool any of the people any of the time. And that's one of the beauties of having a meme. It doesn't try to fool any of the people any of the time but strives to convey something to somebody some of the time.

Armed with that truism, you'll have more realistic expectations of what a meme can do for you. And it can do a lot more than a simple logo, even a stunningly beautiful logo, can do for you. A logo symbolizes your company. A meme symbolizes what your company can do for its prospects. A meme, even with all its simplicity, can be startlingly eloquent.

Show and tell

Examining some logos of the past, a few of which qualify as memes, we come across Prudential and its rock, Traveler's and its umbrella, and Allstate and its hands. Notice that all three of these companies are insurance companies. But that's not the point. The point is that these memes have been in use for decades and are as fresh today as the day they were created. This must be true of your meme as well. Unless you're ready to commit to it and make it part of your overall identity, one that is instantly recognizable, it's not going to do much for your profitability.

What makes your offering contagious

When creating your meme, don't ignore what makes your product or service idea contagious. You want your meme to propagate, much in the manner of a computer virus. Depending on which media you employ, your meme can spread quickly or slowly across a small niche, quickly or slowly across a whole society, or even spread and then vanish overnight, as in the case of companies that left their memes in the dust in a quest for something new — not realizing that newness is not a particular ally of profitability and is often its enemy.

Measuring the potential market for your product or service will remain as essential as ever. With marketing memes, the susceptibility rate depends not just on design, package, name, and advertising but also on consumer age, income, product function, and previous meme exposures. Memes are a new tool for marketing, but they still require time-honored quantitative analysis.

One of the newest memes

One of the most powerful — and newest — memes is a simple two-word statement on many an Internet banner. The words "click here" are so powerful that response rates soar 10 to 40 percent when they are included on a banner. "Click here" and "click now" are especially potent on Internet banners because those banners are clicked by fewer than one-half of 1 percent of the people who view them.

The meaning is crystal clear: people respond to being told what to do. Says one Internet expert: "To the extent that you can hold the customer's hand and let them know what you expect of them, the probability of the action you want happening significantly increases." In fact, a call to action is more effective than ever among today's harried consumers. The simple truth is that most people respond more if somebody asks them to do something than they do if nobody asks. "Click here" is a meme you should seriously consider if you're using banners online. Make people's decisions for them when you can. If content is king on a Web site, it enjoys an even more elevated position when it comes to a meme.

The difference between logos and memes

Before I end this chapter, I'll elaborate on the difference between a logo and a meme. A logo has four components: color, type, content, and size. A meme has only one component — content — whether it is online or offline. And if you begin your quest for a dynamite meme, that's a good starting point. Think content before involving yourself with the details of color, type, and size. If the basic idea behind your meme is clear and powerful, those details will take care of themselves. I doubt whether Uba the caveman was at all cognizant of the color, type, and size of the meme he saw in the cave. It was the content that fired his imagination, and caused a change in his behavior, and influenced human culture.

The U.S. Postal Service conveys its content with an eagle, representing speed and America. Ocean Spray conveys its content with words that create a rocking sensation and a wave curling over the right side. That does a pretty good job of getting us to remember the name, but not of convincing us to buy the brand.

If we examine the problems with logos — some of which are memes, but most of which are not — we discover design errors, the same types of errors that should be avoided with memes. Be sure your meme does not make these mistakes:

The lines are so thin that they disappear in some publications.

Your meme's dependence on color renders it useless in the yellow pages and in newspapers.

It is so abstract that many people won't understand it.

It is not really appropriate for your business because it exaggerates.

It seems amateurish because it uses the wrong proportions for most applications.

It is so busy that people glance away from it.

It employs a fad typeface that will soon be old-fashioned, which is cool only if you want to be perceived as old-fashioned.

By using visual clichés, it makes people think you're a cliché.

It displays an utter lack of imagination — hardly a confidence-builder.

It is confusing, and nobody likes to be confused.

It is remarkably beautiful but conveys zilch about your offering — a common error that can interfere with your profitability.

Steer clear of these common errors, and you'll be well on your way. Focus your meme on the content you wish to convey. Express an idea. Do it as simply as you can. And as the designers go to work on your meme, watch carefully to make sure they don't replicate the common errors made on logos. Your job as a meme-minded guerrilla is to put yourself in charge of the content, and your art director or a hired gun in charge of the color, type, and size. A meme is more than a logo and has a much harder job. That's why guerrillas are more important to marketing than mere art directors — unless you can locate an art-directing guerrilla. The easiest place to find one, now that you have a technique for producing ideas, is right in your mirror.

6

The Myths of Marketing Creativity

▶ ▶ ▶ *Eliminating Ten Obstacles*
to a Successful
Marketing Campaign

T RUE CREATIVITY is rarely found in marketing. That's because the entire concept of creativity in marketing has long been enshrouded in a body of myths that lead creative types woefully astray. I can easily feel the agony of misguided business owners who have wasted billions of dollars believing in the myths rather than the realities of marketing creativity. Their belief in mythology has interfered with their ability to create memes.

Those who create marketing for them think of themselves as artists when they should perceive themselves as businesspeople who use creativity to generate more business. That will happen only when they free themselves from the bondage of the mythology of creativity. The best way I know to liberate them is to make them aware of the myths so that they will no longer be trapped by their worship of false idols.

Although there are many myths that misguide creative types, ten spring to mind as the most damaging of all.

Myth #1: Marketing messages should be communicated from the company's point of view

As I've stated and restated, marketing messages should be created from the point of view of the prospects and the customers. You'd never walk into a room and say, "Here I am! Let's talk about me. Let's talk about what makes me wonderful. Let's talk about what makes me tick. Let's talk about my family, my friends, and my dreams. Let's talk about my history. Forget everything else. Let's just focus on me. Listen to all the great things I can tell you about myself."

Just as you'd be greeted by yawns and quickly departing guests if you said such a thing, most marketing evokes the same response because it's guilty of the same self-absorbed focus. Visit almost any Web site and you won't read much about yourself, but you'll probably be confronted with a river of information about the company. Yawn.

When people are besieged by such information, they click away from the site, change the channel, turn the page, switch the station, or toss the mailing piece. They want to see things from their own point of view, not the point of view of your company. If you want prospects to learn about your company, talk about them. When they see how interested you are in them and how much you can improve their lives, they'll probably want to learn more about your company. But if you leave the starting gate by talking about yourself, you'll probably never make it to the finish line — which is where they purchase what you are selling.

Always keep in mind that they'll make that purchase because of themselves, not because of you.

Myth #2: When great marketing makes people aware of your company, they are more likely to become your customers

I'm very aware of cancer and obesity, of war and pain. Does my awareness make me want these things? It does not. Aiming strictly for awareness is shooting well short of the target. But many highly paid people who create marketing materials feel that awareness is the name of the game. I hope for your sake that this is true of your competitors. As a guerrilla, you want much more than mere awareness.

To be sure, you need awareness, but you need a whole lot more than that. As my ex-boss Leo Burnett, founder of one of the world's great advertising agencies, used to say, "If you want to draw attention to yourself, just come downstairs with your socks in your mouth."

The point is that it's pretty easy to generate awareness. But that's not nearly enough. You want to alter human behavior so that people part with their money to purchase your offering. If you think that mere awareness will accomplish that, be prepared to feel frustrated each time you see your profit-and-loss statement.

Myth #3: Recall will lead to profitability

Consumer research continues to prove that there is no correlation between recall and success. Once people remember you,

you've led them onto the right path, but recall must lead to the sale, not stop short of it.

Granted, it is much simpler for you to make your marketing memorable than to make it motivating. But guerrillas do not take the easy way out. They know that simply being remembered isn't nearly enough to make the sale. They realize that people must remember them, but more important, they know that people must want what they are selling. So they create marketing materials that are remembered but also trigger a purchase. Both factors must be present: recall and motivation. When you see somebody come downstairs with his socks in his mouth, there is no question that you remember him. But do you feel compelled to buy something from him as well? I doubt it.

Myth #4: If people like your marketing, they'll want to buy your product or service

Once again, research shows zero correlation between liking your marketing and wanting your product. And there are case histories galore of people loving the marketing but not buying the product or service being marketed. Many marketers have run TV commercials that were attention-getting, memorable, and loved by the viewing public while, at the same time, sales of their offerings plummeted. People were entertained and amused by the marketing, but when they had a problem, the last thing they wanted was a belly laugh. They wanted a solution, and they wanted it fast.

I'm not saying that if people love your marketing, they'll ignore you. I'm only pointing out that your prospects may love your marketing but not necessarily want to consummate the courtship.

Love is extremely important in marriage, in your life's work, in parenting, and in the pursuit of your pleasure, but it is unimportant in your marketing. It is a basic human desire to love and be loved, and many people who create marketing try to create the kind that will be loved, perhaps in an unconscious effort to be loved themselves. But you can be sure that the Beatles were not referring to marketing when they sang "All you need is love."

Alas, the desire to be loved is the starting point for many a marketing campaign. That's like entering a race facing in the wrong direction. No matter how fast you run, you're going to lose. People love themselves, and if your offering can feed into that love, you're off to a good start. But if your goal is to make people love your marketing, unfortunately you may succeed at that goal — and not at the more appropriate goal of raising profitability.

I personally am not in love with Betty Crocker — even though she is a pretty good meme. But I'm head over heels in love with her Pop Secret popcorn. Here's why. My friends used to complain that the popcorn I served at my Monday night poker games often had unpopped kernels. Pop Secret ran a series of TV commercials telling me that every kernel popped. That's all I needed to know to be wooed away from my old brand of popcorn to Betty's brand. I don't remember whether I loved the TV commercial, but I loved how it provided me with a solution to my problem.

Perhaps the most amazing aspect of this tale is that I viewed the commercial only one time before going to the supermarket and purchasing Pop Secret popcorn. Throughout this book and my past books, you'll hear me laud repetition to the skies, telling you that it is one of the keys to great marketing. But here I am admitting that one exposure to a marketing message was enough for me to make a purchase.

The meaning is clear: if you say the right thing to the right person in the right way, you'll win a customer. That is a worthwhile goal. If the people who created Pop Secret marketing merely wanted me to love their marketing, they might have succeeded at that. Instead, their aim was for me to want their popcorn, and they succeeded admirably in hitting the bull's-eye.

I can think of several TV spots that I loved during a past Super Bowl. But for the life of me, I can't remember who ran them, except for one by Mountain Dew featuring one of my all-time favorite musical groups, Queen. Since seeing that spot, I have purchased two CDs by Queen, but not one can of Mountain Dew.

Myth #5: Your marketing should change frequently

I'm not sure why this myth started in the first place. Perhaps it was because some marketers did not gain instant results from their first efforts at marketing and kept trying again. But it's most likely that the myth arose because people become bored with the marketing. Of course, sometimes marketing undergoes a major overhaul because there is not a whit of evidence that it is working, and the advertiser has given it his all for several months. That's a valid reason to abandon ship. But all too often, plain and simple boredom is the reason for changing a campaign.

Who exactly becomes bored? Probably not the prospects, because they barely notice marketing and must have a marketing message penetrate their minds nine times to move them from total apathy to purchase readiness. Certainly it's not the current customers; they enjoy seeing marketing for items they have already purchased because it reinforces their purchase decision.

The people who become bored are the people who created the marketing, the people paying for the marketing, and the close friends and families of those people. They pay close attention to the marketing and quickly reach their boredom limit.

The truth is that marketing should put forth a consistent identity and a consistent visual presentation. Headlines and copy can change. Illustrations and prices can change. Web sites can change. Even offers can change. But guerrillas are loath to change their graphic personality, their tag lines, and their media. They are especially reluctant to change their memes.

One of the major allies of marketing is repetition. One of the biggest keys to successful guerrilla marketing is commitment to a marketing campaign. These factors should be your cue to leave your marketing alone. Give it a chance to sprout wings and fly. Don't clip those wings before your marketing has become airborne. And whatever you do, don't clip them while your marketing is in flight.

Myth #6: Your marketing will stand out in the cluttered field of messages and motivate the purchase because your offer is so enticing

Because we are all bombarded with marketing coming at us from all sides, especially online, it's more difficult than ever for your marketing to be noticed, let alone to be motivating, regardless of the strength of your offer and the desirability of your benefits.

That's why *consent marketing* is growing so rapidly these days. This type of marketing, when properly conceived, does not go for the sale immediately but instead merely goes after consent. Ask people to be open to your marketing efforts and to give you their consent to receive more marketing materials. Those who give their consent are truly torrid prospects. Those who don't are telling you to save your money and direct your marketing to someone else because they are just plain not interested in what you have to say. Don't resent these people. Appreciate them for enabling you to cut your marketing budget while directing the funds you do invest to truly interested prospects.

It's the growing clutter of marketing messages that has led to this explosion of consent, or permission, marketing, so clearly described by Seth Godin in his groundbreaking book *Permission Marketing*. He expands even further on this idea — and on viral marketing — in his newest book, *Unleashing the Ideavirus*. Seth considers most marketing to be what he terms "interruption marketing" and suggests that you use it merely to secure consent.

As an example, he cites the case of the owner of a summer

camp in New York State, Camp Erehwon. The woman running the camp advertises in the camp directories, which appear in the backs of many magazines. But she does not attempt to sell her camp, simply to get people to send for her video. She also has a booth at camping shows, but again, she does not try to sell the camping experience at her booth. Instead, she tries to get people to request her video.

When people watch that video, do you think they see an attempt to sell the camp? They do not. Instead, the video strives to get people to request an in-home presentation. It's during that in-home presentation that the sale is closed — not only for the child of the parents requesting the presentation, but also for his or her brothers and sisters, schoolmates, and friends — and for several years. It takes a whale of a lot of patience to see this process all the way through to the end, but the payoff is so huge that the patience is a worthwhile investment.

By asking people only to request a video, the camp owner is able to break through the clutter of marketing . . . and to save money at the same time.

Here's another good example of permission marketing. A chiropractor operating in San Diego noticed that the yellow pages there were loaded with display ads for chiropractors. Viewing them as a prospective patient might, she was pretty overwhelmed at the claims they made, and she realized that this might confuse a prospect checking the directory. So she took out a smallish ad, with yellow type reversed out of black type. Her headline read: "Free telephone consultation on how to select a chiropractor." Because this was foremost on the minds of many prospects, they immediately called her number. She told them the things to look for in a chiropractor, then said her practice offered all of those things. Small wonder that the ad broke the bank for her. But don't be surprised. She took advantage of the clutter rather than becoming part of it.

Myth #7: People will behave realistically

The real truth is that people behave according to their perception, and perception is far more important in marketing than reality. In fact, according to the business author and guru Tom Peters, perception is all there is. People make purchases according to their beliefs rather than according to the facts. They perceive their own truths, and guerrillas know that truths are more powerful than facts anytime.

Just what exactly is a belief? There are actually five different conditions that we call belief. The first is *perception,* which refers to awareness. The second is the gut feeling that we sometimes call a *notion.* The third is *opinion,* which is a firmly held notion. The fourth is termed *belief* and is really a firmly held opinion. And the fifth is *conviction,* which is a firmly held belief. Notice that none of the five variations on the concept of belief has anything to do with reality.

Another business guru, Anthony Robbins, says: "Most people treat a belief as if it's a thing, when all it is is a feeling of certainty about something." A belief is a feeling of certainty, not a statement of fact. The finest product or service isn't an automatic success until it is perceived as the finest by prospects. Until they are certain that it is the finest offering available, the facts are meaningless.

True, sometimes the facts and the perception are the same, but very frequently they aren't. When Sony introduced its beta

TV system to vie against the VHS system for use in videocassette recorders, most experts could easily see that the beta system was superior. But better marketing by the VHS companies caused the beta system to lose the battle for consumers. The facts did not speak for themselves. Perception won out over reality.

The same is true for Microsoft, which rode to glory with its Windows software even though Apple had been using Windows features for years. Again, experts familiar with both Microsoft and Apple will tell you that the Apple is the better, more functional and versatile, and simpler of the two systems. But perception again beat the pants off reality because Microsoft beat the pants off Apple — through superior marketing. Reality favored Apple. Perception favored Microsoft. The winner, as always, was perception.

Guerrillas realize that perception is reality. They understand that there are two realities in life. The major one is illusion. The minor one is reality. The closer the two are in your own life, the wiser you are, the better primed for success.

A key to mastery is to recognize each reality for what it is. Buying into illusion and mistaking it for reality is delusion. That delusion is no illusion. To a lot of people on earth, *illusion is reality*. In fact, to most of them, it's the only reality. But guerrillas who have mastered marketing are blessed with the ability to distinguish between illusion and reality, and with the wisdom to control both.

Myth #8: Humor is beneficial to marketing

Humor actually gets in the way of marketing because people remember the joke more than they remember your major message. Marketing improves with repetition, but humor most assuredly does not. It quickly becomes stale, transforming repetition from an ally into an enemy.

So humor ends up making people laugh rather than making your cash register sing. Humor falls into the category of "leech marketing": it sucks attention away from your offer. It detracts from your meme — unless your main purpose with marketing is to entertain and amuse your prospects. Few products or services have attained leadership in their categories because they employed humor. As much as the Energizer Bunny, a wondrous meme, makes you smile, keep in mind that Duracell, which rarely puts even a hint of a smile on anyone's face, outsells Energizer year after year. If people want a battery that is going to last, they turn to Duracell, which they perceive as meaning business, rather than to the cute little bunny that makes them giggle.

I'm the first to admit that humor is just the ticket if you're selling a comedy club, a comedy album, a comedian, a funny movie, or a book of jokes. But probably because many marketing people are embarrassed to come right out and market, they aim a lot of their marketing messages at the laugh rather than the sale. After all, it's a lot easier to make people grin than to make them buy.

Some marketers, such as Miller Lite and Volkswagen, have used humor effectively. But take my word, they are the exceptions to the rule that humor gets in the way of effective marketing. When someone entrusted with the task of creating marketing materials runs dry on motivating ideas, she or he often resorts to humor. But guerrillas know that humor in marketing is a refuge for the unimaginative. The truly imaginative steer clear of it and direct their imagination to generating profits.

Myth #9: Repetition makes marketing boring

The truth is that, by getting through the conscious censors and into the unconscious mind, repetition makes marketing effective. Repetition may be the single most powerful factor in successful marketing. Don't judge your marketing by your own boredom level or that of your coworkers, associates, friends, and family. They pay rapt attention to your marketing, so it's natural that they'll become easily bored.

But your prospects have many things to do besides pay close attention to your marketing. Instead, they ignore it in droves. That's not necessarily good, but it definitely underscores the need to repeat it over and over. The person in charge of deciding when to change your marketing should not be yourself but the person who reviews your cash flow. That person is not likely to become bored with a message that consistently creates profits.

This one myth may be more responsible for the money lost in marketing than any other factor. Creative types in marketing see their mission as creating marketing rather than creating profits. Perhaps they feel guilty when they see their same messages repeated over and over. To assuage that guilt, they recommend major changes in a marketing program. I shudder when I think of it, but these are not bad people — only misguided. And I would have been the first one guilty of the same crime when I was working in ad agencies. But hey, I was younger and less informed in those days. Please forgive me.

Just keep in mind that the cartoon characters Snap, Crackle, and Pop are unquestionably senior citizens, yet they're still as fresh as the day they were born. Rice Krispies have been snapping, crackling, and popping for decades. Sales of Rice Krispies show anything but boredom on the part of consumers. Do you suppose this happy state of events would prevail if Snap, Crackle, and Pop had been abandoned after a year or two? We both know it wouldn't.

To prove how deeply I believe in repetition, I'll tell you one more time that commitment to a marketing plan is the key to marketing success. And I'll remind you that commitment to a meme is what will give that marketing plan its magic and power.

Myth #10: Featuring low prices is creative marketing

Even though low sale prices are detrimental to your bottom line, they generate enough sales to be addictive and dangerous. You feel good for a short time, but that's it. No product category in America is led by the lowest-priced brand. A whopping 86 percent of Americans say there are factors other than price that influence their purchase decisions. Because so many marketers are focused on instant sales and short-term gains, they fall prey to the temptation to cut prices.

But when they do that, they are also cutting their profit margins. And at the same time, they're attracting the worst kind of customers — those who respond to low prices above all else. These are disloyal customers who are quickly won away by the company offering even lower prices. You can't build a profitable business on disloyal customers. With price-oriented marketing, you are training people to wait until you have a sale. There's an old saying in marketing that goes like this: "There will always be someone smart enough, or dumb enough, to sell for a dollar less — which means you're playing a game you can't win." As Bagger Vance says of golf in the movie *The Legend of Bagger Vance,* "You can't win at golf; all you can do is play it." The same is true of cutting prices in a quest for marketing creativity. You can't win at it. All you can do is play it. And as frustrating as golf can be, at least it's more fun than losing money regularly.

With a truly creative marketing campaign, you can cut back on your marketing and still enjoy robust sales. But with price-oriented marketing, if you cut back on marketing, you lose out on sales. When everything else is equal, then the lowest price may win out. But people buy because of value — and price is only one component of value.

If you are in the market for a new TV set and see an ad for one that is priced lower than any competing set, you may visit the store. But when you learn that the TV set has no warranty and was made in Rwanda, you may think twice. It's pretty doubtful that you'll make the purchase. Price would soon lose its luster. Your prospects are a lot like you. Price alone won't cut it for them.

Concentrating on your quality, service, convenience, value, expertise, or reputation will energize your marketing more than price ever could. And it will attract the kind of customers with a high lifetime value, ones who are not quickly wooed away by the first competitor who allows them to save a buck.

If price were so important, nobody would be driving Mercedes, Cadillacs, Lexuses, or BMWs. The highways would be dominated by Yugos. As you can plainly see, price is not omnipotent. It kills profit margins, and it attracts price shoppers. But it is rarely the basis for a wildly successful long-term marketing campaign.

Instant sales do not equate with brilliant marketing. Instead, instant sales are like heroin. They make you feel great at the outset, but dependence on them leads to addiction. And who wants to be addicted to lowering their profit margins? The short term looks gorgeous. The long term looks disastrous. And the only treatment program for this kind of addiction is found in the bankruptcy courts.

Your job, as a guerrilla, is to attract long-term, longtime customers, people who will patronize your business for reasons other than to save a few cents. These are the kind of customers who build a foundation for a profitable and successful business.

You'll attract them and keep them with memes that instill confidence in your company. You may attract them but you sure won't keep them if you gained their business solely with your low prices. That may be what some of them look for. But you can be sure that some business that offers even lower prices will take them away from you.

Instead of directing your creative energy toward communicating how much you can discount your price, you'll be better off seeking to understand the true nature of creativity. You will find that understanding in the next chapter.

7

The Truth About Creativity

▶ ▶ ▶ *Invisible to Most Marketers,*
   Including Your Competitors

T HE CONCEPT OF CREATIVITY is more than fifty
thousand years old and has always been an inherent talent of *Homo sapiens*. Michael Ray, a Stanford professor who teaches a course on creativity, says that creativity resides within everyone. He believes that people have trouble
tapping into their creativity, not because it doesn't exist, but
because their creativity is being suppressed by what he terms
"the voice of judgment" — what I've called "the inner censor."
That's what gets the blame for destroying self-esteem.

Professor Ray believes there are five qualities of creativity
— intuition, will, joy, strength, and compassion — and that
four tools stimulate those qualities: faith in your own creativity, absence of judgment, precise observation, and penetrating
questions. He and I agree wholeheartedly that creativity is not
one great eureka moment that produces a brilliant idea. Instead,
it is a way of life.

Almost every creative professional knows very well that
true creativity is not the result of inspiration but comes from

hard work and focus. I've authored or coauthored twenty-nine books so far, and not one of them has arisen out of a moment of inspiration. If I waited for that flash of inspiration, I'd still be laboring over page one of my first book. The idea is to create by reaching deep into yourself, not to wait for a bright light to flash inside your head. If you do, you're in for a long, dark wait.

Job description for guerrillas

Your job as a guerrilla is to come up with a winning meme — one that identifies your business and communicates something about the quality that you offer, expressed in terms that suggest a benefit. If you're looking for creativity heaven, you'll find it right inside of yourself. And you'll see that your meme not only is the result of your creativity but serves as the nucleus of your creativity for all your future marketing.

Would the great artists, musicians, dancers, and writers have been creative guerrilla marketers? My guess is that they would have — because they did not wait for inspiration but instead knew where to find it inside of themselves.

Dotcoms and memes

A powerful meme would be of extreme value to a dotcom company because it would make that company's offline marketing far more memorable, motivate people to access the company Web site, and demonstrate the primary benefit that the company offers. But many dotcom business owners are too wrapped up in technology, looking for their inspiration outside of themselves rather than within. After all, it's outside of themselves that technology has always resided. But the rules are different with guerrilla creativity: if only they'd look long and hard enough inside of themselves, they'd discover the true source of creativity.

Shhhhhhh!

In the midst of ferocious telecommunications wars and nonstop telemarketing, all the phone companies have been striving for a point of difference. My guess is that some copywriter in some ad agency was one of many working to give his or her client an edge. Research showed that one of the benefits that could be offered by a phone company was clarity of sound.

That copywriter most likely pondered this concept and then tried to recall how people refer to clear sound. "So quiet you could hear a pin drop" came to mind. That spurred the birth of Sprint's meme, a graphic depiction of a pin dropping next to a telephone. As with many memes, it did require a bit of explanation, which Sprint provided with its TV commercials.

Since that time Sprint has been using its meme wisely and consistently, in true guerrilla fashion. Ideally, the company will be able to stay with it for a long time, or at least until research shows that clear sound has become taken for granted. Unlike the short-lived meme Y2K, the pin dropping could be a meme with longevity — the best and most powerful kind.

The tale of Sprint is a tale of creativity in action. You can be certain that the Sprint copywriter was not aiming to win awards or accolades. Instead, the motivation was to communicate a meaningful benefit to consumers, something instantly communicated by the visual of a pin dropping. In just a flash, viewers and readers got the point — no pun intended. This kind of creativity is rare. But it's the kind you'll need in our increasingly competitive marketing environment.

Because creativity is so misunderstood in marketing circles, astonishing sums of money are wasted. Truly creative marketing does not have to be attractive but should come on strong to key prospects, attractiveness be damned. It takes into consideration the lifetime value of a customer rather than the instant gratification of a quick sale.

The lifetime value of a customer

Just what is the value to you of each customer over his or her lifetime? This is a crucial number for you to know because it helps to determine how much you're willing to spend to acquire a new customer. Equally important, it makes you realize how much it costs to lose a customer once you've got him.

Federal Express is one of many companies that focus on the value of a customer. If a midsized company sends thirty packages a week at $25 each, that's $750 a week, or $18,750 a year. If a customer gets angry over one $25 shipment and switches his business to a competitor, Federal Express loses thousands of dollars. That's why every Federal Express supervisor is authorized to grant a $100 refund on the spot, no questions asked, for any delayed shipments. One hundred dollars is a very small price to pay to keep an $18,750-a-year customer. What's the lifetime value of your own customers?

To compute the value of a customer, answer these simple questions:

If you continue to provide acceptable service and quality, how long will the customer patronize your business?

How much will the customer spend in the average year?
Make certain to include the sales increases that are sure to
take place.

What's the total value of this customer?

This number should be engraved in your mind, and you
should share it with all of your employees. It will help you focus on the critical elements of building your business. It will
also remind you to treat each customer as if he or she is the
only customer you have — because if you don't, you may have
no customers at all.

The moment of truth

Truly creative marketing strives to promote recall of the benefit
at the moment of sale rather than in a vacuum. It must be directed to three audiences at once — the "I want to buy right
nows," the "I'll buy pretty soons," and the "I'll probably buy
laters," — for all three audiences can lead to profits.

Guerrilla creativity isn't something that you do. Instead, it's
something that your prospects get. The same is true for quality:
it's not just something you put into your product or service; it's
something your customers get from your product or service.
Guerrilla creativity stimulates understanding and promotes action. Take your mind off of yourself and direct it to your prospects. They're the ones who matter.

To get through to them, you've just got to be different from
the other marketers. Today it takes more effort than ever to
break through the blizzard of advertising, much of which simply copies other advertising that has won awards.

By being aware of this situation, you'll be more apt to know what to do about it. What to do about it is to have your very own meme — yours and yours alone. Your success depends a great deal on your ability to create — or delegate the creation of — a powerful and durable meme for your business.

This is not time-honored advice because memes are so new to the world, let alone the marketing world. But it will become time-honored advice because the effectiveness of meme-power marketing will be demonstrably evident. The sooner you have your own, the sooner you'll benefit. In an increasingly cluttered marketing environment, and one that will soon experience an explosion of memes, seniority counts. The older memes will be far more welcomed and recognized than the new memes on the block.

The specific strengths of each marketing medium

Your success also depends on tailoring your marketing to each marketing medium — for each has its own particular strengths.

1. *The power of newspapers is news.* Marketing that is newsy gets noticed because news is on the forefront of readers' minds. If you can add an element of news to your newspaper marketing, you'll be giving readers just what they're looking for in the first place. The memes in your newspaper advertising should match the memes everywhere else you market. And don't forget that newspapers limit most advertisers' meme colors to black and white, unless the advertiser is willing to pop for color. Be sure that your meme looks as good in black and white as it does in color because you don't want to incur extra charges if you can avoid them.

2. *The power of magazines is credibility.* Readers unconsciously attach to the advertiser the same credibility that they associate with the magazine. They become far more involved in their magazines than in their newspapers, so you can market in magazines knowing that readers will be more open to becoming involved with what you have to say and show. The meme in your magazine ad must be intensely visual, because in magazines and newspapers people get all of their data through their eyes.

3. *The power of radio is intimacy.* Usually radio is a one-on-one situation allowing for a close and intimate connection between listener and marketer. Although in all media you should be speaking to one person at a time, you can do it even more intimately on the radio. Here's where the visual power of your meme goes for naught. The words will carry the day, if they're going to carry anything. The words, music, jingle, and sound effects are the raw materials for your meme. If they closely connect with your visual meme, give yourself a gold star.

4. *The power of direct mail is urgency.* Time-dated offers that might expire before the recipient acts often motivate them to act now. Using this technique requires a bit of restraint on your part: prospects don't mind being pressured occasionally, but they resent it if the pressure is repeated too often. If people know who you are, put your meme on the envelope. If they don't, and you know it's a winning meme, put it on the envelope anyway and give yourself another gold star. Those without gold stars ought to use their meme, not on the envelope, but on the letterhead, brochure, business reply card, and reply envelope.

5. *The power of telemarketing is rapport.* Few media allow you to establish a give-and-take kind of contact as adroitly as

the telephone. Even though the Internet is a bastion of inter-activity, telemarketing was the first to promote and utilize it. As with radio, this is no place for a visual meme, but one where a verbal meme can stimulate warm feelings of acquaintance-ship. When you say it, be sure it doesn't sound like blatant marketing.

6. *The power of brochures lies in giving details.* Few media allow you the time and space to expand on your benefits as much as a brochure. The prospect who asks to see your bro-chure is really saying, "Tell me all the details about why I should purchase from you." Your meme should be one of the stars of your brochure, appearing right at the start, at the end, and possibly in other places as well. Your brochure is where you get to expand on the implied promise made by your meme.

7. *The power of classified ads is information.* Nobody in their right mind actually reads the classified ads except for those searching for data. And these days, with increasing num-bers of magazines adding classified sections and with so many free classified sites online, the guerrilla pays more attention to classified ads than ever before. Except in rare instances — such as online classified sections with graphic capability or display classified sections in print publications — visual memes are pretty worthless in the classified world, but verbal memes call attention to themselves, being an island of familiarity in a sea of strangers.

8. *The power of the yellow pages is even more information.* In the yellow pages, prospects get a line on the entire competi-tive situation and can compare. No medium gives you as much opportunity to go one on one with your competition. Never for-get that people "let their fingers do the walking" (a powerful meme in itself) to get data, not to see pretty pictures. So be sure

your yellow pages ad gives them the data they seek and does not waste their time and your money on appealing graphics instead of cogent words. Although the yellow pages lets you capitalize on the power of both verbal and visual memes, unless you're willing to invest in color, your meme will appear in black and yellow. Clients have told me that the investment in color for the yellow pages is usually a wise one. If you're not going to make that investment, however, be sure that your meme looks like a winner in yellow and black.

9. *The power of television is demonstration.* No other medium lets you show your product or service in use, along with the benefits it offers, like television. Online marketing is growing stronger every day and will continue to gain power, but TV is still the undisputed heavyweight champ of marketing. That's why many guerrillas use it to direct viewers to their Web sites. As media become more and more sophisticated, guerrillas combine one medium with another to gain leverage and visibility. Of all the places where memes can strut their stuff, TV is the best. It lets you show your meme, say your meme, sing your meme, animate your meme, breathe life into your meme, and spotlight your meme. If I were a meme, I'd sure want to be a TV star.

10. *The power of signs is impulse reactions.* Signs motivate people to buy when they are in a buying mood and in a buying arena. Signs either trigger an impulse or remind people of your other marketing, or both. Memes become even more important in an environment where signs are used, such as in retail establishments. Ideally, prospects see your meme on a sign and quickly remember what it stands for because they've seen it in the other media.

11. *The power of fliers is economy.* They can be created, produced, and distributed for very little and can even bring about instant results. Essentially, a flier is all headline. Not much room or need for details. Say what you have to say, and do it quickly. Or else. A meme can prove invaluable to you when brevity is necessary. If you market with circulars, I predict you'll be delighted that you have a meme.

12. *The power of billboards is in reminding.* Billboards rarely do the whole selling job, but they're great at jostling people's memories of your other efforts. Memes can work wonders on a billboard, where you have the chance to say only six or eight words, frequently even fewer. Once you have a meme, you'll see more and more opportunities to put it to work for you — showing it and saying it. Billboards represent one of the most obvious forums for displaying your meme.

13. *The power of the Internet is interactivity.* On the Internet, you can flag prospects' attention, inform them, answer their questions, and take their orders. You can initiate and carry on a continuing dialogue with visitors to your site. You can combine words and graphics to increase the potency of both.

Many marketers use the Internet the same way they use radio and television, magazines and newspapers, and overlook the immense power of interactivity. If it's relationships for which you're striving, no medium allows you to enter into them as easily as the Internet. Whole messages can simply be forwarded or transmitted verbatim. Particular parts of a message can be separated from the original and propagated on their own. In addition, because of the rapidity of transmission, experimenting with the spread of new ideas can be done over a realistic time scale.

There is a natural affinity between memes and the Internet. As with TV, the Internet offers a gamut of display possibilities for your meme, from dynamic streaming video to static banners.

Not all media were created equal

Guerrillas are aware of the specific powers of each medium and design their marketing so as to capitalize on them. Their awareness gives them a greater return on their marketing investments than if they created marketing oblivious to these special strengths. By capitalizing on their wisdom, they get the very most that each of the media has to offer. Adjusting the message to the medium is an art form and a necessity.

It's not very difficult to see how a meme can add strength to the inherent strengths within each medium, though try as I might I still can't see how a visual meme helps much in telemarketing. But it's pretty obvious how it aids your cause across the rest of the media spectrum.

Not all media were created equal. Guerrillas are quick to take advantage of these inequalities to increase the effectiveness of each weapon they use.

The truth about creativity embraces the differences between the forms of media and inspires guerrillas either to direct their ad agencies properly or to be their own creative geniuses.

Transforming yourself into that kind of genius will be a lot easier now that you know the truth about creativity. Applying your enlightenment to your marketing is a different story entirely, one that will be told when you turn the page.

8

Breaking Through the Clutter

▶ ▶ ▶ *Creating Dynamite*
Marketing Materials

G UERRILLAS KNOW that their marketing does not exist in a vacuum but must compete for attention, not only against their competitors but also against everybody vying for the time, attention, and disposable income of readers and viewers. Guerrillas know how to make adjustments to face up to the realities of marketing today: more clutter than ever, and a need for more wisdom than ever before to stand out in it. Once again, a meme will stand you in good stead by being immediately recognizable and by communicating your prime benefit.

If you're running print ads, try pasting them into the publication before you submit them. Do they stand out in the clutter? Do they call attention to themselves? Prospects don't view ads one at a time but as part of a mass of marketing communications. It's smarter for you to view your marketing through the eyes of a prospect than through your own eyes. If you have a Web site, before putting it up on the Net, check out other Web sites, especially those of your competitors. After all, that's what your prospects will do.

More and more marketers are discovering that powerful memes are the cutting edge of cultural and economic evolution. They change minds, alter behavior, shift perceptions, and transform societies, not to mention individual purchase patterns.

It's becoming clear that as we plunge further into the Information Age, whoever has the memes has the power. Right now corporations have the power. They beam their memes, if they are wise enough to have them, into our brains at the rate of four thousand ads, brand logos, and marketing thrusts per day — and counting.

That's a whole lot of clutter. No matter how cogent your message, breaking through that clutter and getting noticed is going to be a monumental task. Making a sale is even tougher if the real battle is simply to gain attention. Your ally in this battle will be your meme.

The meme you choose will not only spearhead your guerrilla marketing attack but serve as the cornerstone. It will help you stand apart from the competition — and don't forget that the competition is everybody who markets. The competition is also the news articles in the print publications, the music and talk on the radio, and the programs on the television set. How ever will your marketing capture the attention of an inundated crowd? It's not an easy task, but a meme will be your answer. A meme can alter the entire scene, not by communicating everything to everybody but by communicating something to somebody. The world will not be changed, but some people will want what you are offering.

Those who use memes properly have altered everything from the food we eat to the way we get from point A to point B, from the way we beautify our bottom lines to the way we browse the Internet. Most important, they seem to dictate the way we spend or invest or lose our money.

Meme control

Savvy and well-heeled corporations also control many of the means of the spread of memes: the TV and radio stations, movie theaters, magazines, newspapers, and online services. That's precisely why meme warfare is growing ever more intense. The next revolution will be, as the media guru Marshall McLuhan predicted, "a guerrilla information war." That battle has already been joined. It is being fought in the streets with signs, slogans, banners, and billboards. But it will be won in newspapers, on the radio, on TV, and online. It will be a no-holds-barred propaganda war of competing perceptions and alternative visions of the future. Memes will be at the forefront for the victors.

The big corporations have their ad agencies and PR firms, their designers and writers. And let's be sure not to overlook their multimillion-dollar budgets. But those deep pockets may not be enough. Small and midsized businesses with shallower pockets, much like yours, have the Internet — the biggest and best meme disseminator ever invented. Thanks to it, you also have a globally linked network of artists, designers, hackers, and multimedia whiz kids.

Your USP in a brave new world

To determine your own meme, after being fully cognizant of what's on your prospects' minds, delve into what the famed ad agency founder Rosser Reeves, in his landmark book *Reality in Advertising,* termed your "unique selling proposition," which has become its own meme — USP. Your USP is all about the claim you can make that others can't. That's what makes it unique. Because it is directed at provoking the specific action of making a purchase, that makes it all about selling. And because it tenders an offer of a positive benefit in exchange for a purchase, that makes it a proposition. Without a USP, your meme may be dramatically underpowered. With a USP, it is ready for action. And it is ready to be heralded by a meme. In the past, a USP was enough. In the future, it will need a companion meme to achieve its full strength.

Where to start?

Begin your quest for a meme with a marketing strategy, a simple paragraph describing what you want your marketing to accomplish. It makes no sense at all to learn about memes if you don't have a marketing strategy into which the meme can breathe life and vitality.

To develop a winning meme, first tune in to what some experts term your client's "radio station." Its call letters are WII-FM, which stands for "What's In It For Me?" Guerrillas are aware that most people are motivated by self-interest, so offering a clear, concise solution to their needs is key to getting a positive response.

Be sure also to tune in to and embrace the lingo that your prospects use, since incorporating their terminology into your meme can make it more relevant and memorable. Compose your meme around your USP, your competitive advantage, that appealing aspect of your product or service that clearly differentiates it from competitors and provides value to the client.

Your USP should be a specific differentiation or promise concerning quality, service, or price. Examples include a lifetime guarantee, the largest selection, a low price guarantee, a generous return policy, value-added services, proprietary information or specialized knowledge, a track record of performance, and industry expertise. A USP can be something that competitors don't offer, something that competitors do offer but have not exploited, something that you are not — such as the UnCola — or something that you are — such as the largest provider of software to the legal industry.

What your prospects want to hear

The best way to break through the clutter is with a USP that tells your prospects exactly what they want to hear. They want to hear about themselves, and if your product or service shows them how they can better enjoy life on earth, you'll get right through that clutter and into their hearts.

They want to hear that you're aware of their needs and aware of their problems, that you have solved problems such as theirs before, and that you can provide them with a superb value. Know what else they may want to hear? The sound of their own voice. They need to be assured that you're listening to them and will continue to listen to them. Notice that they do not want to know much about you. But they are intensely interested in themselves. You must share this interest if you're going to get their business. Do they want to know what you give? Not much. Do they want to know what they get? You bet they do.

What people get

Robert Middleton of Action Plan Marketing in Palo Alto, California, knows a thing or three about memes. Spend a few moments reading his take on them. We can tell that Robert is a guerrilla because first, he counsels other guerrillas to focus their marketing messages on what the prospect gets instead of on what they do. That almost seems too simple, but it makes all the difference. And it's absolutely astonishing that so few small-business owners — and big ones as well — actually "get it."

Like me, Middleton urges business owners to turn their marketing messages into memes. He asks pertinent questions of small-business owners:

Are you frustrated trying to communicate about your business?

Do you do great things for your customers, but just can't talk or write about your products or services in a way that gets any attention, let alone any response?

Directing his message to service professionals, he tells them that they want to get more clients, but that to reach that goal, they first need to get noticed and create interest in their services.

One voice in a big crowd

To stand apart from the crowd, you need to do more than just tell people about what you do. You need to communicate your unique talents and abilities in terms that are both meaningful and compelling to prospective clients.

Middleton hits the nail on the head when he poses this query: "You've probably been told that it's a good idea to develop a business name, tag line, elevator pitch and headlines. But have you worked on messages like this for hours and they still don't have any oomph?" Then he tells you the same truth that I've been telling you: "You can start creating marketing messages that hit home every time."

According to meme-meister Middleton, powerful marketing messages aren't only about the content of your message. Just as important is how you structure your message. That's the key that almost everyone misses.

Although Richard Dawkins gets the credit for identifying and describing memes, he limited his investigation to genetics and didn't say a word about memes in the context of marketing. The Australian author Geoff Ayling was one of the first to build a strong case for the use of memes in marketing and advertising. Truth be told, he believes that the meme is the missing piece of the marketing and advertising puzzle. And considering how much money has been wasted on ineffective marketing, it's hardly shocking that he refers to marketing and advertising as a puzzle.

"A meme," he writes, "operates through the process of chunking complex concepts or ideas down into a simple, easily communicable unit." In the same way, marketing messages can be constructed as memes to communicate the benefits of a product or service more quickly and easily.

That's why it's necessary these days to apply marketing memes to virtually any marketing message. The obvious reason: people will understand you more quickly, and as a result, you'll attract more attention, interest, and response, not to mention comprehension. Without that ease of comprehension, you're sunk.

Memes and elevator pitches

A meme is far more important than a mere elevator pitch. In the elevator, you have up to thirty seconds to tell your story. With a meme, you have mere seconds, probably three at the most. And you're lucky to get them. So I urge you to get one and stick with it. Take your mind off of zippy slogans or phrases. Just strive for clarity, simplicity, brevity, and benefits, all wrapped up in a few words — or a combination of words and images, or simply an image. Great marketing memes make a direct and memorable connection whether they are words or images or a combination of the two.

What a meme is not

To apply your native creativity to the challenge of breaking through the clutter with your own meme, it's important for you to understand a marketing meme by knowing what it is not. A meme is neither a meaningless slogan nor a clever play on words. Have you ever seen a headline on a billboard that confused you? Of course you have. Who hasn't? That's a meaningless meme. Memes should never confuse. They should clarify. With a meme, you unconsciously say, "I get it!" When it's not a meme, you unconsciously say, "Huh?" — or more likely, you forget it entirely. People do not want to work hard to understand marketing. Like a truly good joke, a meme hits home immediately and everybody gets it.

Slogans, headlines, tag lines, and other marketing messages aren't necessarily memes. Usually they're just clever phrases built on a play on words, or they're so general that they communicate very little. "Overnight delivery" isn't much of a meme. It didn't require and doesn't demonstrate one iota of creativity. But the slogan "When you absolutely, positively have to have it overnight" built a multimillion-dollar business. Your challenge is to create memes for your business that communicate the benefits of your service just as powerfully as Fedex did.

Verbal memes

When creating verbal memes, keep in mind that it doesn't take many words to make your meme. In fact, many of the most famous are merely adages:

"The squeaky wheel gets the grease."

"What goes around comes around."

"We hold these truths to be self-evident."

"Of the people, by the people, and for the people."

"Ask not what your country can do for you. Ask what you can do for your country."

"Read my lips."

"Go ahead. Make my day."

The best verbal memes mention the name of the product. "Promise her anything but give her Arpège" is more on-target as a meme than Coty's "Want him to be more of a man? Try being more of a woman!" Coty's verbal meme could be for any product, but Arpège's is unmistakably for Arpège.

Here are more examples of powerful verbal memes, some long gone:

"Nothing comes between me and my Calvins": This meme could only be for Calvin Klein.

"Please don't squeeze the Charmin": The resurrected Mr. Whipple speaks for Charmin tissue and for nobody else.

"See the USA in your Chevrolet": This meme encourages more driving as well as doing it in a Chevy.

"Have a Coke and a smile": This is one of many memes used by Coca-Cola over the years, and one of the few that mentions Coke's name.

"There's a Ford in your future": This meme was used for a long time by the Ford Motor Company, as if you didn't know.

"We do chicken right": This KFC meme didn't mention its name but did mention its primary product. "Finger-lickin' good" was one of the company's early memes, and for the life of me I can't see why they dropped it.

"How do you spell *relief*? R-O-L-A-I-D-S": This meme names both a benefit and the marketer.

"Mmmm, good . . . mmmm, good . . . that's what Campbell

soups are . . . mmmm, mmmm, good!": Not only does this meme state a benefit and mention the name, but it works well with music.

"Schaefer is the one beer to have when you're having more than one": This meme is clearly directed to beer lovers, not beer dilettantes.

"I wish I was an Oscar Meyer wiener . . .": This meme conveys the fun of Oscar Meyer hot dogs as well as their name.

"Winston tastes good like a cigarette should": This meme kept Winston up among the leaders until the Marlboro Man knocked it from its perch.

Off-the-mark memes

Now let's examine some memes that were off the mark, primarily because they didn't mention the name of the product and could have been for anyone.

"I can't believe I ate the whole thing": This meme generated a lot of laughs for Alka-Seltzer, but no profits. Somebody hit the bull's-eye on the wrong target.

"Does she or doesn't she?": This famous and successful verbal meme didn't mention Clairol. Still, a lot of women were motivated by the line to purchase L'Oreal.

"America's most gifted whiskey": Four Roses' cute and clever meme could be applied to a host of booze brands.

"We bring good things to life": Because General Electric's meme could be for many other companies as well, GE spends a fortune reminding you that it is the company doing the talking, but guerrillas rarely have a fortune. At least at the beginning they don't.

"Ring around the collar": A dandy statement of the problem, this meme nevertheless didn't give a hint that it was Wisk laundry detergent that removed the ring.

"Getting there is half the fun": Marketed by Cunard Cruises, this truism could have applied to lots of other companies as well.

"Quality is Job #1": This verbal meme was used in conjunction with the Ford logo, so people knew who was talking. But as a stand-alone meme, it is too anonymous.

Memes, both verbal and visual, animated and live action, are not as easy to pin down as I'd like them to be. For instance, *"Plop plop fizz fizz,* oh, what a relief it is," doesn't say a word about Alka-Seltzer but was very successful in its day. I still think that company is sorry it dropped its *"Plop plop"* and its Speedy character. There's no question that both were memes and that both helped Alka-Seltzer earn hefty profits.

The same is true for American Express's "Don't leave home without it." This verbal meme could be for any credit card company, but American Express has invested enough money to lay claim to it. Guerrillas rarely have that luxury.

One more example of the complexity of companies using memes is AT&T's "Let your fingers do the walking." Still in use, this meme was first brought to life visually, through the image of fingers walking across a surface. But the verbal meme seems to have been dropped, allowing the visual meme to do all the heavy lifting. When should memes be used and when should they be dropped? When should they be visual and when should they be verbal? These are good questions, and just a year or so ago they were never asked. Now businesses are asking them and seeking answers.

When to use memes

A meme, used in a seriously capitalistic marketing sense, can be used any time you need to communicate effectively about your business. It communicates an obvious benefit quickly and effortlessly, and it stimulates a response, either immediately or sometime in the future, because it's so easy to recall. People may see your meme in an ad or a banner, or hear it on the radio or television, and when they see it again in a store, or even on a direct-mail postcard, they have no trouble remembering why they should purchase what you are selling. That means that memes may not generate a sale instantly, but they can generate a sale eventually.

To apply what you've learned about memes to the real world, begin by asking the crucial question: "What do my prospects get as a result of using my product or services?" Don't concern yourself with the wording or the graphics quite yet. Merely brainstorm a number of sentences or visuals that capture the essence of your key benefit.

The anatomy of a meme

Here's an example of the birth of a meme. Initially you might come up with: "Our clients have problems with employee conflict, and our services help reduce that conflict while building cooperation and trust." Hardly a meme, but the core idea is there in this overly long sentence. You try to pare it down to its essentials: "We reduce conflict while building cooperation." Closer, but no cigar.

You try again and come up with: "Reducing conflict and building cooperation within organizations." Kind of ho-hum as a meme, and also pretty darned wordy. The final meme, used as a tag line, is: "Building cooperation within organizations." This is simple, benefit-oriented, and easy to remember. The graphic might be an organization chart within a heart. It conveys both organization and cooperation. It looks like a meme, sounds like a meme, communicates like a meme, and serves as a meme.

Field-testing your meme

But is it any good? Will it break through the clutter of information? Testing will tell you the bottom-line truth. Once you've developed what you consider a meme, you must test it to see whether it communicates your core message. How do you know whether or not it does?

Here's how. You notice that when you say or show it, people ask the right questions and want to know more. Ideally, they even want to make a purchase right here and right now. You might also test it as an audio meme. When someone asks what you do, say something like: "I have a company called Working Diplomacy. We help build cooperation within organizations."

If most people say, "That's interesting, more companies need that," or, "You ought to talk to our human resources director," there's a very good chance you have a winner. But if many people ask, "What do you mean?" or, "Why do companies need that?" you need to go back to the drawing board.

After making enough trips to that drawing board, you may

develop a meme that you can board and ride to victory. That means your job is just starting. A meme isn't just a nice thing to have. It's the core expression of your business purpose and strategy. So use it everywhere you possibly can. Put it in the tag line of your business card and stationery. Use it as a headline in an ad, answer the phone with it, include it in your e-mail signature, and put it on the home page of your Web site and every other page as well. Put it in the yellow pages, on television, on the radio — in every medium you employ to reach your target market.

The whole idea of a meme is that it helps prospects understand quickly and easily how you can help them, so include it in every single piece of promotional material you use and in all the marketing activities in which you engage.

Connecting your company closely with your meme is like riding a bicycle. It's virtually impossible to lose your balance once you've learned how to do it, and it gets you to exactly where you want to go. Better still, it gets your prospects there as well. I am hardly writing about rocket science when I write about memes. Although the word is relatively new, the concept is crystal clear: a meme should identify your organization and say something about how people benefit by doing business with you. Do they hear sound so clear with Sprint that they can hear a pin drop over the phone? That meme identifies an organization and conveys a benefit. Do they see Mercury carrying a bouquet of flowers? That means FTD delivers flowers in a hurry.

When you see little round candies dancing, who else but M&Ms has told you that they melt in your mouth and not in your hands? With both a visual meme and a verbal meme, M&Ms has earned both of its Ms.

Memes and eyes and ears

Seeing a visual of a pin dropping tells you a lot, but it doesn't relate the entire story. Whatever you do, don't fall prey to that misleading maxim that one picture is worth a thousand words. Although it is undeniable that we receive the majority of our information visually, neurologists tell us that what comes through our ears stays in our minds for five full seconds before it begins to fade. But what comes to us through our eyes is gone in less than a second. I guess that's nature's way of protecting us from information overload.

Eyewitnesses can almost always agree on exactly what they heard, but few can agree with certainty on what it was they saw. By the time they do realize the significance of what they saw, that critical second has passed and their clear memory of that vision is gone with the wind. One picture is worth a thousand words? I don't think so.

Our populace has a burning desire to make difficult things easier to understand. This helps explain the 1,335 ". . . for Dummies" books. It also helps to demonstrate the dire need for memes in marketing: they make a difficult premise very simple to understand.

The poet within you

Some experts believe that the poet who dwells within you will come up with your meme. They report that while journalists seek to inform us and creative writers strive to entertain us, it is the poets who change how we see the world. With stunning simplicity, they form within our heads new mental images and a whole new way of thinking. Their perspective helps us barrel right on through the clutter.

They stimulate our imaginations as well. Guerrillas know that if you engage the imagination, you can take it wherever you want. Where the mind has repeatedly journeyed, the body will surely follow. People go only to places they have already been in their minds.

There is a poet within each of us, and by turning off our inner censor, we can more easily access that voice. "Reach out and touch someone," another AT&T line, sounds more like poetry than advertising. I recall my eyes misting over when viewing some of the TV commercials in which it was used. Bottom line: did those spots motivate me to call my sister in Chicago? Answer: they sure did.

"If I have only one life to live, let me live it as a blonde!" was created by a closet poet working as a copywriter for Clairol. Even "A day without orange juice is like a day without sunshine" sounds as much like poetry that touches the heart as it does like advertising that touches the wallet. The Florida Citrus Commission sold a whale of a lot of oranges with that poetic verbal meme.

"I dreamed I stopped traffic in my Maidenform Bra" sounds more like the work of a poet than of an industrialist. And "Nothin' says lovin' like something from the oven" actually was a poem for Pillsbury. At least it rhymed. So did Texaco's "You can trust your car to the man who wears the star." But don't get the idea that all memes should rhyme or be poetic. They can, but they sure don't have to.

Some of the most powerful memes come not from the poet within but from the patriot within. "You've come a long way, baby," was about the women's liberation movement far more than it was about Virginia Slims cigarettes. Women rallied around the brand as a political statement as much as for any other reason. And the shape of the cigarette, described in its name, was another reason women were attracted to it. The shape was a meme for the brand.

One of the reasons it is so valuable to think like a poet but write like a patriot is that you can enlist your heart to come to the aid of your mind. You can stop operating on the intellectual plane and move up to the feeling level. When a former cabinet member, a Republican, was asked to join a Democratic government, he asked his five-year-old son for counsel. He posed the question: "What's more important, your heart or your mind?" The son quickly replied, "Your heart." When the father asked why, the son said, "Because your heart is never wrong."

It's for that reason that I urge you to open your mind to tapping your emotions in a quest for your meme. Your heart may be a font of meme ideas. People who look into their hearts for their marketing ideas give their prospects a new perspective. These people go where few have gone before, especially in the realm of marketing.

They also go to where other people have been before. Hardly anyone wants to be the first to try anything. An old adage implores us to "be the first on your block to use it!" People feel far more comfortable being tenth on their block. And being one-hundredth on their block gives them even more of a reason to relax. If you want to draw a crowd, remember that nothing attracts a crowd better than a crowd.

Social proof

Exploiting this comfort zone is called "social proof." It's a clutter-breaker supreme. You must remind your prospects that they will not be pioneers. They know that pioneers get arrows in the back of their necks. So you must reassure them that others have taken the trail to which you are pointing, that others have very successfully benefited from using your product or service. Why do you suppose McDonald's says, "Billions and billions sold," at all its outlets? Not to brag, that's for sure. Why does McDonald's show its golden arches throughout many of its TV commercials? Because McDonald's feels that the arches have meme power even though they say nothing about the products. The arches have so much meme power that many people around the world have made McDonald's, Big Macs, and Happy Meals part of their own identity. They actually define themselves as Big Mac people, or McDonald's people. Kids think in terms of Happy Meals when they get hungry, a fine thing for McDonald's.

As a quarter-pounder (hold the cheese) kind of guy, I gravitate toward our local McDonald's, but I think Burger King may be a bit better at the meme game. Its "flame-broiled" meme, showing a burger sizzling over flames, addressed the issue of fried foods while teeming with appetite appeal. Its "Have it your way" provided the solution to still another problem identified by research and made a compelling promise.

The importance of an identity

One of the most powerful needs in a human being is the need for an identity. One of your tasks — and your meme will help you accomplish it — is to make your offering part of a person's identity.

I recently received a gift: a T-shirt that said "Pizzaboy.com," heralding a new online pizza delivery Web site. The people who sent it were trying to get me to make them part of my identity, figuring I'd wear the T-shirt, it would be seen by my friends, and I'd be motivated to patronize the site. Giving me the T-shirt didn't accomplish the entire task of putting me in their corner, but it did aim me in the right direction.

In my little county in California, where the vast majority of computer users have Macs instead of PCs (unlike the rest of the nation), people often identify themselves as Mac users, for Apple has made its way into their identity, and they are proud to proclaim it. Harley-Davidson has accomplished the same thing. And so has the Grateful Dead — ask any deadhead. When people ask, "Is that your final answer?" you know they have made ABC's *Who Wants to Be a Millionaire?* part of their identity.

Saturn automobiles are attempting to do the same thing and seem to be succeeding, based on the attendance at gatherings for Saturn owners. Kids by the millions have made Mickey Mouse and Disney part of their identity, and Budweiser is part of the identity of many a beer-drinker, judging by the hats and T-shirts popular with this crowd.

I have to warn you that the marketing environment is a hostile one for those who blithely market while remaining oblivious to the need to establish such a strong relationship that your company becomes part of your customers' identity. When you see umpteen books about relationship marketing, you're seeing proof of the growing awareness of the need to make a business part of a person's identity.

Joining the inner circle

A good place to connect with your prospects in the hopes of making yourself part of their identity is their inner circle. You must join the inner circle that surrounds each prospect. That circle includes the person's family, friends, car, toothpaste, coffee, sports teams, soft drink, beer, breakfast cereal, clothing, community, and a lot more. Most people have developed an intimate relationship with all of these elements of their inner circle and often describe themselves as Pepsi lovers, Wheaties eaters, or Forty-Niners fans.

The products have actually become like family, through a long-term relationship based on familiarity and trust. Because you want to become part of the inner circle of as many prospects as possible, it's important that you know three things about it:

1. *The inner circle is the basis of all repeat business.* People do not buy products within their inner circle casually. They make the purchases as part of their routine behavior. Memes open the door to the inner circle.

2. *You can't gate-crash your way into the inner circle.* You must earn an invitation to be part of it, then be consistent with your marketing. An inner-circle relationship is based on attraction, not coercion. Remember that attraction happens when you become attractive, not when you come on like gangbusters. That means your meme need not hit a prospect over the head as much as caress that person.

3. *If you're not in the inner circle, you can be sure that your competitors are.* So when you market to prospects, you

are saying, "Stop buying from those whom you love and trust. Instead, buy from us. We're complete strangers, but hey, we want your business." The moral: your offering must be worthy of inclusion in the inner circle. It must compare favorably and actually be better in some way than what the competition offers. This refers to quality, service, and value. Can you communicate any of those attributes in your meme? Perhaps you can if you try.

Why companies lose business

I hope you don't create a killer meme, use it to attract an impressive number of new customers, then lose those customers by ignoring them. A meme might add them to your customer list, but it's you who must be creative enough to keep them there.

Guerrillas know that the main reason companies lose business is apathy after the sale. They know that the opposite of apathy is follow-up. People stop purchasing a brand or patronizing a business because they perceive a sense of indifference on the part of the company. Deep in their hearts, they want that company to care about them. If they are ignored, they do not feel cherished. If they do not feel cherished, they will seek someone who adores them. Follow-up keeps the love light burning. To lose a onetime customer is bad enough. But to lose a regular customer is tragic.

You've got to stay in touch with customers by mail, phone, e-mail, special events, personal visits, anything it takes to prove to them that you want to keep them satisfied forever. Just seeing your meme is often enough to make people feel that you still care about them, and guerrillas come up with many ways to communicate it — from decals to posters, from postcards to T-shirts, from calendars to Christmas cards. Having a meme is part of the battle. Using it is something else again. Creativity reigns in both areas.

Strategic creativity

Just as marketing is paramount for business success, creativity is paramount for marketing success. The business and communications environments have changed so dramatically that there is no longer room for mere creative creativity, and there is a crying need for strategic creativity, aimed at making prospects part of your identity. Creative creativity is largely indulgent and irrelevant, while strategic creativity draws attention, gets down to business, makes its point, and influences consumer buying decisions.

Winning memes are the result of strategic creativity. They withstand the passage of time and never appear dated. Because memes grow stronger with time, longevity should be one of their key characteristics. Using memes in your follow-up marketing is simple and inexpensive and reminds people of why they began buying from you in the first place.

CNN led the way in making memes part of a customer's identity by keeping its name onscreen regardless of what it was telecasting, except during commercials, when other memes were shown. The CNN meme, consisting only of the letters CNN, occupied a tiny corner of the screen, but it served as a constant reminder to the viewers that they were watching CNN. Today numerous networks do the same thing, keeping their meme onscreen and constantly reminding people of the channel they are watching. I'm not sure whether Ted Turner knew he was employing a meme in the right way, but his intuition told him that showing his network name was the right thing to do.

The rarity of memes

Today I scoured about five magazines, including a few devoted to marketing. I was on my never-ending search for memes. I came up empty.

I watched TV almost nonstop during the 2000 presidential election, which, from the perspective of 2001, looked like the real Y2chaos. Yes, I was fascinated with all of the news analyses, but I was shocked at the absence of memes in the TV commercials.

I admit to being a big fan of Regis Philbin and (gulp!) even of *Survivor.* Sure, I enjoy the shows, but I rationalize my TV watching as necessary to my quest for memes. My house is one of the few in which you can talk during the programming but must be silent during the TV commercials. I've enlisted the help of my wife and friends in my search for successful memes.

The good news is that they are incredibly rare — which means that the competition is asleep at the wheel and the ground is fertile for guerrillas who know the power of memes and can apply their creativity to their marketing. You can thank your lucky stars that you are now among them.

9

Creative Positioning
and Enduring Patience

▶ ▶ ▶ *Owning a Position That Lives
        in the Minds of Your Prospects*

YOU SEE THIS — ".com" — and suddenly you know
for certain that it has something to do with the Internet.
In a relatively short time, ".com," or "dotcom," has
come to mean the Internet. It's a meme that has become known
to computer users throughout the world. Obviously it doesn't
have to take eons for a meme to become recognized. Patience,
which is normally required, wasn't necessary to establish the
dotcom meme in the public mind.

The same is true for an old typewriter meme — @. Ten
years ago, @ meant "at," as in twelve avocados @ $1.00 each.
Today it still means "at," but in a different context, as in jay@
jayconradlevinson.com. In neither the dotcom case nor the @
example does the meme promise a benefit, but it does signify
an instantly recognized idea that almost everybody understands.

Some of the most successful users of memes have been magazines. You see a fancy-looking man with a top hat and a monocle, and you know it means *The New Yorker* and all the wit and sophistication represented by that magazine. A bunny head says *Playboy* magazine to you and conveys all the sexual and literary innuendos that go along with the publication.

The Golden Gate Bridge? It's a meme that has come to stand for San Francisco. The Sun Maid girl with her basket of fresh raisins — a meme for Sun Maid Raisins. Chiquita is a visual meme suggesting bananas and also an audio meme telling you to never put her bananas in the refrigerator. "Bananas have to ripen in the heat of the tropical equator, so you should never put bananas in the refrigerator."

The life span of a meme

The last time I heard that meme was when I was about ten years old, but I still remember it. Winston cigarettes have been gone from the market for nearly two decades now, and yet most people can complete this sentence: "Winston tastes good like . . ." This is proof that memes have an exceptionally long life span — if you stick with them and make them part of all your marketing materials. They are so powerful and inherently long-lived that they are remembered long after the products they represent have faded from existence.

On your mark, get set . . .

Of course, at the starting line of meme creation is the prime benefit you offer. You must pay attention to your product function and the needs and wants of your prospects. Remember that a lot more than color is involved in creating a meme. You must take heed of your overall design, package, name, and advertising media — in addition to the age of your prospects, their incomes, and their previous meme exposures. A wildly successful meme on MTV may sit there and wither on NBC. An ideal meme on television might be a total loser in the yellow pages. The best memes cross all media and cultural boundaries.

Guerrillas have long known that a product is best marketed through an assortment of media. So your meme may have to work online, in magazines, on T-shirts, on the radio, and in a direct-mail piece. That's not an easy job, and it's exactly why small-business owners have long been flummoxed when it comes to developing and committing to a meme.

Memes and evolution

As a species, we have coevolved with our memes. Imagine a group of early *Homo sapiens* in the late Pleistocene epoch. They've recently arrived with the latest high-tech hand axes to show their *Homo erectus* neighbors how to make them. Those who can't wrap their minds around the new meme are at a disadvantage and will be out-evolved by their smarter cousins.

Meanwhile, the memes themselves are evolving, just as in the game of Telephone, in which a message whispered from person to person is slightly misreplicated each time. Selection favors the memes that are easiest to understand, to remember, and to communicate to others. The ability to understand and communicate complex memes is a survival trait, and natural selection should favor those who aren't too conservative to understand new memes.

Your winning personality

It's important that your meme communicate not only your benefit but also your company personality. The ad great David Ogilvy says:

> Products, like people, have personalities, and they can make or break them in the marketplace. The personality of a product is an amalgam of many things — its name, its packaging, its price, the style of its advertising, and, above all, the nature of the product itself. . . . When you choose a brand of whisky, you are choosing an image. Jack Daniel's projects an image of homespun honesty and thereby persuades you that Jack Daniel's is worth its premium price.

Jack Daniel's advertising plays the meme game to the hilt. When you look at advertising that depicts laid-back old Tennessee boys who, with all the time in the world, are just waiting around for that "Tennessee sipping whisky" to mature, you're taking a powerful mind virus, an identity meme, on board. Having been downloaded into your mind, that meme works silently beneath the surface, efficiently shifting your perception and shaping your belief about the product.

The all-powerful Jack Daniel's meme, conveyed in photos and a slogan, shows that bourbon drinkers aren't really buying bourbon. They're buying an identity, a feeling about what they believe the product to be.

They are buying a meme. It's true that a regular customer may now buy Jack Daniel's because he or she enjoys the way it tastes, but that original purchase was most likely meme-motivated. That's why the brand identity must be factored into your meme with the same aplomb employed by the distillers in Tennessee.

Because of the simplicity and clarity of the Jack Daniel's meme, it stands above a lot of other bourbon marketing, which seems to market the product category rather than the product. The same is frequently true of airlines, four-wheel-drive vehicles, hotels, and a host of others. These companies are oblivious to the fact that a strong meme represents their specific product, and they blindly market their product category instead — to the dismay of their accountants and the delight of their competitors.

Positioning made simple

The way around this all-too-common dilemma is to understand brand positioning. It is not about targeting your product as much as owning an idea in the minds of your prospects and customers. Positioning is misunderstood by those who invest their budgets in creating brand or product category awareness when they should be communicating their own product's competitive uniqueness. Geoff Ayling says that this is like using a sumo wrestler to move a boulder when all that's really required is a kid with a crowbar.

The authors Jack Trout and Al Ries, in their landmark book *Positioning: The Battle for Your Mind,* define positioning more precisely:

> According to Positioning theory, the human mind contains slots or positions which a company attempts to fill. This is easy to do if the position is empty, but difficult to do if the position is owned by a

competitor. In the latter case a company must "reposition" its competition if it wants to get into the mind.

When Marlboro cigarettes were enjoying year after year of steadily rising sales, based largely on its cowboy meme, the company owned that position, having aligned its brand with the legendary folk heroism of the West. Other cigarette brands quickly tried to emulate Marlboro, using cowboys in much the same way. But each time they ran an ad, Marlboro sales rose again because people had learned to equate cowboys with Marlboro.

Me-tooism is rampant in marketing. Creative people fall all over themselves trying to copy a meme that a competitor has created, always to no avail. Guerrillas do not copy. Guerrillas innovate. They ask themselves hard questions before developing their meme:

Are we the experts?

Are we the fun people to do business with?

Do we make shopping easy?

Are we the acknowledged specialists?

Are we the largest in the land?

Do we have the best reputation?

Are we the most expensive?

Are we famous for superlative service?

Are we known for our endless selection?

Are we the most reliable?

Are we the fastest?

Do we offer the most online convenience?

Do we offer the freshest?

Can we deliver our products within thirty minutes?

Advanced guerrilla creativity requires you to ask the right questions, come up with the honest answers, then create a meme around the answer that gives you a true competitive advantage, an answer that can dictate your positioning.

You are going to own a position in the marketplace regardless of how you market. Advanced guerrilla creativity suggests that you take control of that position, for if you don't, the public will do it for you. When that happens, either cross your fingers or consider going into another business, for your future will be dictated by those competitors who own a position that they have carefully planned and marketed.

Worst-case scenario: you market, advertise, promote, train, invest, polish, and perfect — and to most people, including your prime prospects, your brand means nothing whatsoever. The marketing world teems with worst-case scenarios.

A meme to the rescue

That's why a meme must come to your rescue. A meme shows your target market exactly what you stand for, exactly what makes you different, and exactly why your product or service should be the brand of choice.

Dell computers are all custom-made, shipped directly to customers, and not available from retailers. Does the computer company offer a chance to test its product at a well-stocked computer store? It does not. Even better, it grants all purchasers a free thirty-day trial. Dell has no warehouse. It doesn't even have a visual meme. But it does have a theme line: "Your very personal computer company." And it sure does own a position. Computer owners worldwide are aware of Dell through its on-line and offline marketing.

Compare Dell with Compaq. Compaq's company theme line, "Quality and performance without compromise," can re-fer not only to Compaq but also to Dell, Apple, Microsoft, United Airlines, Buick, Sears, or Timex. Not one word of that theme line is unique to Compaq. The idea is to have your com-pany and brand name become synonymous with something your customers and prospects value highly — and that some-thing must be unique.

Meaningful versus meaningless

Often a meme takes the form of a literal description, which is a lot more effective than a meaningless slogan. Evian says, "Nat-ural spring water from the French Alps." Stolichnaya Vodka says, "Genuine Russian vodka." Hardly the words to make your heart sing or send you scurrying to the store, but still, a lot more potent than "quality and performance without compro-mise."

Literal descriptions live up to their definition — descriptive. Meaningless slogans also live up to their definition — mean-ingless. But meaningless slogans are so endemic in the market-ing world that it's enough to cause you to pour yourself a Stolichnaya, washed down with an Evian chaser.

Positioning in a competitive environment

Trout and Ries offer advice on how to position your brand in a highly competitive environment: "If you can't be first in a category, set up a new category you can be first in." When Orville Redenbacher wanted to introduce his popcorn, he was pretty overwhelmed by the number of competitors. But he didn't let that stop him. Instead, he created a new product category, evident in the name of his brand: Orville Redenbacher's Gourmet Popping Corn. Suddenly there was a whole new product category, and it was dominated, to nobody's surprise, by Orville Redenbacher, who had created it in the first place.

Tylenol, rather than being deterred by the ocean of headache remedies available to the public, came up with an ultra-powerful verbal meme, based on research showing that aspirin can cause minor stomach bleeding: "Tylenol — for the millions of people who should not be taking aspirin."

Bingo! Bull's-eye! Goal! Tylenol rode that meme to the point where it displaced aspirin as the number-one painkiller nationally. Today it is the best-selling pharmaceutical product in America.

Asking for permission

Now that I'm on the topic of best-selling items, I feel compelled to call your attention to one of the best-selling business books of the new millennium, even though it was published way back in 1999.

Sometimes the student becomes the teacher. That's exactly what happened to me when my former student Seth Godin, co-author of three books with me, wrote his own *Permission Marketing: Turning Strangers into Friends and Friends into Customers.* It changed my entire outlook on marketing and can dramatically change the beauty of your bottom line. Although I touched on consent marketing earlier, learning advanced guerrilla creativity calls for more than a mere overview.

Seth has enlightened me to the presence of two kinds of marketing in the world today. The first is the most common, the most expensive, the most ineffective, and the most old-fashioned: *interruption marketing.* A TV commercial, a radio spot, a magazine or newspaper ad, a telemarketing call, or a direct-mail letter interrupts whatever you're doing to state its message. Most people have never paid very much attention to it, and now they give it less attention than ever because there is so much of it and because they have learned unconsciously to filter it out.

The opposite of interruption marketing is the newest, least expensive, and most effective kind. It's called *permission marketing* — prospects give you their permission to market to them.

It works like this. You offer your prospects an enticement to volunteer to pay attention to your marketing. The enticement may be a prize for playing a game. It could be information that prospects consider valuable. It might be a discount coupon. Perhaps it's membership in a privileged group such as a frequent buyers' club or a birthday club. Maybe it's entry into a sweepstakes. And it might even take the form of a free gift. All you ask in return is *permission to market to these people.* Nothing else.

Alas, you'll have to use interruption marketing to secure that important permission. And you'll have to track your costs like crazy, figuring out how much it costs you to gain each permission — easily figured by analyzing your media costs divided by the number of permissions you've been granted.

Once you've embarked on a permission marketing campaign, you can spend less time marketing to strangers and more time marketing to friends. You can move your marketing from beyond mere reach and frequency and into the realm of trust.

Once you've obtained permission from your prospects, your marketing takes on three exciting characteristics. It is *anticipated,* meaning that people actually look forward to hearing from you. It is *personal,* meaning that the messages are directly related to the prospect. And it is *relevant,* meaning that you know for sure that the marketing is about something in which the prospect is interested.

A meme helps to identify you when you are using interruption marketing and it also helps people remember you when you are knee-deep in permission marketing. It symbolizes you, and your prospects will remember you each time they see your meme. After all, they've embraced your story enough to have given you permission to market to them.

Permission marketing is not about share of market, nor even about share of mind. Instead, it's about *share of wallet.* You find as many new actual customers as you can, then extract the maximum value from each customer. You convert the largest number of prospects into customers, using the invaluable permission you've gained from them to accomplish this. You focus your marketing only on prospects, not on the world at large.

The goal of each step is not to make the sale immediately but to expand permission for you to take another step toward it. Who uses permission marketing these days? Record clubs. Book clubs. Marketers who offer a free brochure. Numerous Web sites (including my own at jayconradlevinson.com) offer a weekly report for free — in effect, gaining permission to market to all those who sign up.

The Internet and permission marketing

The biggest boon to permission marketing is the Internet — but only to marketers who treat it like an interactive medium, not like a TV . . . and primarily to those who comprehend the awesome power of a meme.

As clutter becomes worse, permission becomes more valuable. The moral: since only a limited number of companies within a market niche can secure permission, get moving on your own permission marketing program pronto.

To ensure that your interruption marketing is noticed above the hubbub, and as a way to carry it into your permission marketing campaign, use a meme to create the momentum you need. Use it in all the steps of your campaign.

Prospects will see it in your interruption marketing, then remember what it stands for after they've granted permission to you. Each time they hear from you, they'll see that meme, which will continue to implant in their minds the prime benefits that you offer. In time a wave of ideas will flow through their mind when they merely spot the meme — ideas that you have planted, using the meme as the seed from which you will harvest sales.

Come to where the patience is

Shall I tell you why you need patience to make your meme take wings and fly? Try and stop me. Back in the late fifties, Marlboro had the identity of a feminine cigarette and was ranked number thirty-one in sales. The Marlboro brand group called in our advertising agency to help. "Can you help us rise from that lowly position of number thirty-one? Can you change the perception of our brand from feminine to masculine?" Although there were more female than male smokers in those days, men smoked more cigarettes, so they were the target market.

The agency dispatched a couple of photographers and an art director to a ranch owned by one of the art director's friends. They were told to shoot unposed photographs of real cowboys doing what they do on a real ranch. For two weeks they shot photo after photo. While they were there, the writers at the ad agency, Leo Burnett Advertising, came up with a visual meme — the cowboy — a verbal meme — Marlboro Country — and even a theme line — "Come to where the flavor is. Come to Marlboro Country."

When the photographers and art director came back, the photos were developed, enlarged, and tacked to a wall in a conference room. Then the typeset words were pasted on each picture. You saw a cowboy. You saw the theme line. You saw a pack of Marlboro cigarettes. In those days the cowboy had a tattoo on his hand to further instill the idea of masculinity. In the fifties more men than women wore tattoos. These days I'm getting the feeling that more women than men sport them.

These cowboys in the photos were not decorated with a real tattoo, mind you, but one drawn by ballpoint pen and enhanced with a bit of paint. Later the secretary of the Navy wrote to us requesting that the tattoo be removed because young sailors were getting tattoos and getting into trouble at the same time, probably owing to nonsterile needles. Needless to say, the tattoos were discontinued in future ads. We sure didn't want the secretary of the Navy to be giving us a hard time (though it hardly compared to the trouble the surgeon general would give us a few years later). Anyhow, the tattoo was only a minor part of the identity created for the Marlboro Man.

The campaign was presented to the Marlboro brand group, which was so impressed that it agreed to invest $18 million in marketing during the first year. The Marlboro Man, that meme with a western twang, became a cultural icon. He was featured not only in newspapers and magazines, on signs and billboards, but also on radio and television, for in those days it was legal to peddle carcinogens in the electronic media. We even rented the music from *The Magnificent Seven,* my all-time favorite movie, for $50,000 per year.

One year later we flew from our ad agency in Chicago to the Marlboro brand group in New York City. We were secretly hoping for high fives, pats on the back, a slew of compliments, and most of all, a report telling us that Marlboro was now a top-selling brand.

But this was not to be. Cultural icon or not, the Marlboro Man had been largely ignored, and the brand remained mired in thirty-first place. Worse still, focus group interviews indicated that Marlboro was still perceived as a feminine brand!

What was going on here? We had been showing macho cowboys doing macho things in a macho setting, but still, Marlboro was considered a cigarette for females. We had the right visual meme. We had the right verbal meme. We had the right slogan. We used the right music and the right media, and we invested the right amount of money to motivate smokers to switch brands.

What was lacking?

Patience was lacking. Today, as you read this, Marlboro is the number-one selling cigarette in America. It is number one to men. It is number one to women. In fact, of every five cigarettes purchased in the whole world, one is a Marlboro.

But here's the real shocker: since the inaugural marketing, nothing has changed. Marlboro still uses cowboys, still refers to the unspoiled West as Marlboro Country, and still invites smokers to "Come to where the flavor is. Come to Marlboro Country." True, the tattoo is gone. True, cigarette marketing has since been banished from radio and television. So what created the miracle rise in sales?

Giving credit where it's due

Patience with a meme gets the credit. By hanging in there, the Marlboro brand group rode to glory. The meaning is ultra-clear: a wondrous meme used without patience is probably doomed. Your theme line may be glorious, but if you push it impatiently, it'll just sit there. It takes the combination of a winning meme plus extraordinary patience to cash in on the magic of memes.

In this book, I can teach you all about memes in marketing. But can I teach you to be a patient person? I can suggest it, but that patience must come from within yourself. For a meme is only as powerful as the people using it are patient.

Today Marlboro is generally recognized as the beneficiary of the most successful marketing in history. But whatever you do, don't give credit to the cowboy. Give credit instead to the brand group, which recognized the value of commitment to a campaign.

High cathexis and low cathexis

Some product categories, such as shampoo, benefit from very little product loyalty, because shampoo is a low-cathexis product. Cathexis measures the degree of emotional involvement a customer has with a brand. People are not emotionally attached to their shampoo brands, as demonstrated by the fact that women use several types of shampoo each year. They are constantly experimenting and being wooed away from their old brands by the power of the word *new*!

But cigarettes are a different story. They are a very high-cathexis product, smokers being very emotionally attached to their brand. In fact, many of them define themselves by the brand of cigarette they smoke. The people running the marketing show at Marlboro knew that, so they were prepared for very little change to occur in a hurry. They knew that it takes a whole lot longer for a high-cathexis product to attract new users.

Low-cathexis products — such as toothpaste, socks, paper towels, and software — aren't really part of a person's identity, and so marketing can cause brand switching in a relatively short time. But with high-cathexis products, which are often part of people's identity — certain cars, wristwatches, athletic shoes, books — brand switching isn't so commonplace. "I'd rather fight than switch" was a verbal meme used by a cigarette, Herbert Tareyton. A black eye was the visual meme. Although the brand is hardly a market leader, its memes tell us a lot about the cathexis value of a cigarette brand. Fighting rather than switching? Possibly true for some cigarette brands. Almost impossible with shampoos.

You should become familiar with the cathexis level of your own business, be it a product or service business. If people are emotionally involved with offerings in its product or service category, your meme is going to have to work extra hard.

The positioning of Marlboro, which dictated its meme, was not enough. It took monumental patience to ignite the payoff. Positioning and patience get the credit for a marketing story that is now as legendary as the cowboys on which it was based. These attributes are an integral part of guerrilla marketing as well as guerrilla creativity.

10

Why You Need a Meme Now More Than Ever

▶ ▶ ▶ *The Importance of*
Starting in the Right Place

F YOU WERE UBA the caveman, unable to catch a fish with your bare hands, and you saw a meme of a caveman holding a stick with a fish impaled on the end, chances are that you'd do a lot more than merely think that it looked interesting.

If you were a caveman who was cold every night, and somebody showed you how to build a fire, you wouldn't just absorb the information without acting on it. If you were dragging things through the dirt, exerting a lot of energy to get them where you wanted them to be, and somebody demonstrated a wheel to you, you'd do way more than smile and think, how fascinating.

That's why I hope you realize that a meme for your marketing is a major breakthrough in creativity. It's a major advance over a logo or any other traditional marketing weapon. It can propel you from just hanging on to enjoying consistent profitability. With a meme, your marketing can burst through the clutter like a Roman candle. It can separate you not only from your competition but also from the vast majority of other companies that market.

In the barrage of marketing messages aimed at consumers — and who among us is not a consumer? — a meme is not a luxury. It is a necessity. So many businesses, so many offers, so many enticements are being beamed out that it takes something dramatically different to stand out. Finally, the meme has been identified as that something. Consider it in context.

A brief history of advertising

Back in the days of early advertising in the 1920s, integrated marketing was the happening thing. From Pepsodent to Palmolive, from Pepsi to Penney's, the guerrillas of the day integrated advertising with in-store signage, offering samples through club-type memberships and special incentives to prospects through sales promotions. Memes hadn't even been identified yet, but even as late as the 1960s integration was a byword of marketing.

The creative revolution

And then *creativity hit the fan.* The creative revolution, which took hold of advertising in the 1960s, led advertising to become fascinated with itself and lose interest in the client's business. Building portfolios was divorced from building sales. Awards proliferated, but most celebrated clever art and copy, not the ringing of the cash register. Some advertising people would learn the very expensive lesson that being cool is hardly a marketing strategy.

Hey, I saw it happen. I was there. I was appalled. I saw clients force wan smiles onto their faces as they picked up first prizes for advertising while knowing that they had lost 21 percent market share and $34.6 million that year.

I left advertising agencies during this reign of the creativity cult. The loony bin was indeed being run by the loonies. And I was one of them. As a creative director in a creative agency, I worked in the Twilight Zone. So I up and left.

The 1970s and 1980s were characterized by ad agencies obsessively producing ultra-expensive thirty-second TV spots, and anything not related to stylish, creative TV spots was seen as unworthy. But then, in the 1990s, three things happened to bring marketers to their senses.

1. *Mass media fragmented.* Network TV no longer reigned supreme. Small businesses, which were beginning to flourish as never before, could suddenly reach parts of the mass markets, paying just a tiny fraction of the mass media costs, with regional ads in national magazines, zone edition ads in metropolitan newspapers, local commercials on cable TV, and highly targeted direct-mail lists, not to mention the opportunity to market to millions directly over the Internet.

2. *The mass market disintegrated.* The time was ripe for niche marketing. Businesses that couldn't even hope to afford mass marketing in the mass media discovered that by aiming at small rather than large targets, they could easily afford to turn a market on a small scale and enjoy a large-scale return on that marketing investment. With their smaller appetites, many small businesses could become bottom feeders in the new economy.

3. *The economy decimated marketing budgets.* Direct mar-

keting grew. Twenty years ago, 75 percent of marketing budgets went into advertising. Today, with direct marketing through the Internet, mail, and telephone, 50 percent goes into trade promotions, 25 percent to consumer promotions, and a bit less than 25 percent to advertising. Bye-bye, hip advertising. Howdy, profits.

Enter the dragon

The meme is the dragon symbolizing the next generation of advertising and marketing. It is as old as human life on earth and as new as today's technological advance. It will be at the forefront of successful marketing efforts in the present and in the future. In a race, a head start can mean victory. In a competitive marketing environment, awareness of memes in marketing — in your own marketing — can mean the difference between profit and loss. Don't ever say you weren't given a head start.

It makes no difference whether your big guns are fired through magazines and newspapers, radio and television, direct mail and telemarketing, or Web sites and regular e-mailings. Your meme can supercharge your profits even in simple networking functions. A meme can power up your marketing in any media, now and forever. It can help you stand apart, be remembered, motivate human behavior, and be clear with your marketing message at all times.

The concepts of one-on-one marketing and relationship marketing (each term the titles of a superb book) were more than exercises in using marketing in a new way. They influenced the marketing of many businesses and had a dramatic and positive impact on their bottom lines. As did viral marketing, described so eloquently and vividly by Seth Godin in his book *Unleashing the Ideavirus*.

The same is true for guerrilla creativity and its reliance on memes to energize your marketing and move it into a much higher gear. Memes can make all the difference in the world to your marketing efforts.

Six steps to creating a meme

Because of its potential significance to your company, you should begin developing your meme the moment you finish this book. You may have a good idea already. If you don't, you'll have one soon if you remember these six steps:

1. Do your research.
2. Write your benefits list.
3. Determine your competitive advantage.
4. Select the marketing weapons you'll employ.
5. Write your marketing plan. Then . . .
6. . . . develop your meme.

A meme is something you'll need right at the beginning. It's not something you come up with down the road. If it is, chances are you're traveling on the wrong road.

A meme for your marketing arsenal is like an atomic bomb for your fighting arsenal. Firing cap guns, all of your competitors are thrilled by the noise but frustrated by their inability to conquer you and still clueless as to the weaponry of a new millennium. This book is giving you a clue. It's giving you exactly what you need to energize your marketing as never before. It is far more than a theory of marketing: it's a law of human behavior. It's a law you should never break.

Action and marketing

Just as action is the purpose of guerrilla marketing, a meme is at the heart of that action. It should appear on all of your marketing communications, from your business card and stationery to your online and offline marketing efforts. Savvy marketers are constantly looking for an edge in their marketing campaigns. A meme gives you that edge.

A meme simplifies complexities. It clarifies ambiguities. It reveals realities. Once you have a meme, it takes on a life of its own while breathing new life into your marketing. It taps into the emotions of individuals within your target audience. The famed ad man Bill Bernbach has reassured us that it is emotion, not reason, that sways individuals and mass audiences alike. Facts alone just don't do the job. In fact, you probably can't put forth a rational argument in just a few seconds. But you can trigger an emotion if you use a meme. And when you do that, you can really and truly present your company's main benefit to millions of people in an instant.

A meme can be as colorful as a flashing, sparkling Web site or as bare-bones as a small, simple line drawing in a yellow pages directory. Size, as half the planet wants you to believe, does not matter.

What really matters

Ideas matter. Clarity matters. Helping others matters. Empathy matters. Save the bells and whistles for New Year's Eve.

Many people bad-mouth marketing and advertising. They hurl all kinds of insults at it — until they have to market or advertise something. Then everything changes, and they realize the difficulty of effective marketing. They often resort to the tried and true, most of which is now the uninformed and the ineffective. What used to work in the past is impotent now in a world of clutter and complexity.

That's why one of your most crucial starting points is something that will work in today's world of marketing, all over the place, twenty-four hours a day, seven days a week. It's a starting point that wasn't recognized during the last century, even by those who came up with Juan Valdez and Mrs. Butterworth. And it wasn't nearly as mandatory for a company when there was less clutter and life was simpler on all fronts.

But that was then. The present requires different tactics, different weapons. A meme is just the tactic you may need to make the difference between breaking even and turning a glorious profit.

The real competition

Always remember who your real competition is: absolutely everybody who markets. Your meme will help you to stand apart from all competitors as well as your direct competitors.

Not only is it consistent with your original message to use your meme during your follow-up, but your prospects will be reminded of why they were intrigued by the idea of doing business with you in the first place. Just as follow-up is a major component of marketing, your meme is a major component of follow-up.

Guerrilla creativity encourages you to use a meme in your marketing and to think like a long-distance runner. The opposite of that is to ignore memes and to think like a sprinter. Short-term gratification may be yours, but long-term gratification is why you're in business.

Marketing has changed a great deal during the past century. But human behavior has not changed much at all. People still respond to the same emotional tugs, to the same basic appeals, to the same selfish needs and wants.

Pressed for time

Today people are more pressed for time and less likely to devote their precious moments to studying marketing. They want you to get right to the point — specifically, what's in it for them? — and nothing accomplishes that better than a well-conceived meme.

In the old days of marketing it was understood that a business needed a name, a sign, a method of communicating. Next, businesses realized that it helped them immensely if they had a logo, a theme line, a brochure. As time passed, it became apparent that a business needed to advertise in the media that reached its prospects. Now many businesses have gone online — because that's where their prospects have been heading.

With memes now identified and described, the deployment of them should become standard operating procedure for any farsighted company with a firm grasp of the realities of the marketplace. Luckily for you, at first that will be only guerrilla marketing–minded companies — businesses that are quick to react and want to conserve their marketing investment and get the most for their money. That will give you a head start over the many businesses that still operate in the dark ages of the twentieth century.

Wince when you recall that half of small businesses fail. They fail for many reasons, but poor management heads the list, and poor marketing is in the top five. You can't really blame them for failing to use a meme in their marketing, but you can blame yourself if you don't take full advantage of this marketing concept that was born in genetics.

Memes and flexibility

Once you have your own meme, don't feel that it is engraved in bronze: if it's a good meme, it is the essence of flexibility. It springs to life as a simple drawing on a page as well as it does during three seconds of action in a TV commercial. It deftly spins its web of comprehension in the few seconds it takes to glance at a home page or to hear words or music coming from a radio. It changes with time without altering its soul. Aunt Jemima changed her headdress but maintained her identity. Betty Crocker updated her wardrobe but didn't let that interfere with her perceived culinary prowess.

Memes are organic and must function as living entities if they're to spearhead your marketing over the long haul. You plant these organic entities as seeds — nurturing them, paying close attention to them, including them when you fertilize and water your land. Memes are not going to sprout in a hurry but will send out root systems into the minds of your prospects. As you demonstrate your commitment to them, you'll begin to catch glimpses of the results of your agriculture. You'll see your meme seeds bloom and take on a vibrant life of their own.

You'll continue to nurture them, but you'll also begin to harvest. Your crop of prospects being transformed into customers will make for a bountiful and endless harvest. Unlike your farming counterparts in Iowa, you won't have to plant the seeds each year. One serious planting will do the trick, enabling you to focus your energy on harvesting.

Because you'll be making your primary point with your meme each time you communicate in any way, you'll be getting a better return on your marketing investment. There are five logical reasons this is so.

Five reasons why you'll get a better return on your marketing investment

1. Your message will be understood.
2. Your marketing will not be diffused.
3. Your major benefit will be implanted consistently into the conscious and unconscious minds of your prospects.
4. You will waste less of your marketing investment because it will become more effective.
5. You'll be able to make a smaller marketing investment because so little is being wasted.

Combine the new idea of marketing with memes with the new idea of consent marketing, then blend them with the old idea of fervent follow-up and the old idea of personalized marketing, and you have an ultra-powerful formula for making waves with your marketing. Start with a clear marketing plan and the inner conviction that you're going to commit to your marketing plan — and you are primed to get more from your marketing than ever before.

Are memes expensive?

If you think a meme is expensive, consider the meme used by the meme expert Robert Middleton of Action Plan Marketing (easily found online at robmid@actionplan.com). It's simply a seven-word line he uses at networking functions: "I help service businesses attract more clients." It's instantly understood. It's right to the point. It promises a real benefit. And it opens the door to closing the sale. Just think: a spoken sentence at a networking get-together. And some people think marketing has to be expensive.

You attend a seminar. The speaker is cursed with a monotone, uses unnecessary words, and sends endless sentences droning your way. You zone out. A lot of marketing is cursed with a monotone, exaggerates, and sends meaningless sentences droning toward prospects. The prospects zone out.

People pay attention only to what they understand. When you use a meme in your marketing, people will understand you more quickly, and as a result, you'll attract more attention, interest, and response. Prospects will zone *into* your message — because it's about them. Forget those myths of marketing. Just strive for clarity, simplicity, brevity, and benefits, all wrapped up in a simple visual or a few words — or both.

The importance of the connection

Memes will help you make *the connection* that marketing must make. Much of marketing in the past seemed to do everything possible to get in the way of the connection. Creativity was rampant but misguided. It hit the bull's-eye, but on the wrong targets.

Making the connection is paramount. It's the first step in establishing a relationship. Memes are all about making that connection — right off the bat.

If people have to think, even for a moment, about what you mean by your message, they're not going to respond to it and that all-important connection won't be made.

Like a great joke, a meme hits home immediately. But don't make your meme a joke because you know how jokes sound when repeated. Make your meme specific more than funny, clear more than gorgeous, timeless more than trendy, obvious more than subtle. Even if only one person in ten doesn't know what the heck you're talking about, that means one hundred thousand people out of a million won't get the point you're trying to make.

Getting to the point

Do you know the point you ought to be trying to make? Do you know the basis of your meme? No hocus-pocus is involved. Just begin right now, this book in your hand, by asking yourself a simple question: How do I create a powerful meme for my business?

To answer that, ask another question: What do my prospects and customers get as a result of using my product or services? Think of two or three simple sentences that state the heart of your key benefit. Pare the sentences down to their bare essentials. Now try to visualize someone gaining from what you have to offer. Open wide your imagination, but don't let it soar into outer space as much as into the inner space of your prospects' minds.

The fruit of guerrilla creativity is a meme that can lead your marketing parade. Don't let the barriers to creativity get in your way. If you know them, you can surmount them. Barriers to creativity include:

Relying too much on statistics

Always following the rules

Playing follow-the-leader

Thinking conventionally

Judging yourself too harshly

Being too controlled by research

Being afraid of failure

Rushing because of emergency conditions

Expect these barriers. Then hurtle over them as though they never existed. They not only get in the way of your creativity but serve to sabotage your profitability. Memes equate with profitability. Without a meme, your business can be profitable, but attaining those profits is a tougher job. You don't need a wristwatch to tell the time, but knowing the time is a tougher job without one. Why do without a breakthrough when it's so simple and inexpensive to use it?

What marketing is all about

All you've got to do is keep in mind that marketing is no longer about price or quality or even service. It's not about reputation or location. Instead, marketing is about *ideas* — and memes are expressions of ideas, the simplest expression possible.

As Seth Godin reminds us in *Unleashing the Ideavirus*, we live in a world where consumers actively resist marketing. So it's imperative to stop marketing at people. Is a meme really and truly a form of marketing? It most assuredly is. And right now, to be depressingly candid, marketing is all there is. You don't earn a whole lot of profit with better shipping or manufacturing or accounts payable. But you can earn sizable profits with better marketing, because marketing is about spreading ideas, and ideas are all you've got left to compete with.

That means the future belongs to the people who unleash memes on their prospects. This is not a bad thing. In fact, this is great news to those who shudder at the clutter, who create banners praying that they'll be noticed, who lack the big bucks to mount a comprehensive marketing campaign.

But big bucks are not the key to spreading a great meme. A big imagination is all that's really necessary. A big imagination can create a meme that leads to big profits. Guerrillas know that they should not concentrate on sales or traffic, response rates or volume. The only game they are playing is the one in which the winner amasses the most profits. Profits are their goal. You'd think the pursuit of profits would be elementary to business owners. It is not.

According to Forrester Research, only 20 percent of fifty leading online retailers expected to turn a profit in 2000. Just 18 percent more expected to be profitable in 2001. It's becoming painfully obvious that many of these sites will never turn a profit, and that they're hoping to last long enough to be acquired or to sell their stock. Alas, even a meme might not be enough to rescue these companies, many of which are going under because they started out in the wrong direction, failing to focus on profits in the first place. It's one thing to hope for profits your third year. It's something else not to focus on profits at all. Some dotcom companies have been guilty of focus failure.

A McKinsey and Company study found that the vast majority of online retailers are not only unprofitable but actually losing money on every sale. Without even computing the cost of advertising and clicks, these sites have discounted their prices so significantly that the contribution margin from each sale is negative. The average online drugstore, for example, loses $16.42 on each and every sale, before computing the cost of traffic. Can a meme substitute for an overreliance on price? As much as I believe in memes, I don't think so.

What went wrong?

The reason so many sites have been led into this sad state of affairs is that many of them believe that keeping prices low is an effective customer acquisition tool. There's probably no less effective, more costly, and more confusing strategy than cutting your prices to the point where you lose money on each sale. Memes can't do much about absurd pricing. Add to this mess the obscene cost of acquiring customers online, estimated by the Boston Consulting Group to be more than $80 a visitor — that's *visitors,* not customers. Now you can see the huge hurdle these sites are going to have to clear to be profitable. Memes can help them conquer some of those hurdles, but certainly not all of them.

Memes and integrated marketing

What do guerrilla creativity and memes have in common with a boomerang? If you throw a stick, it flies about 30 feet. Frank

Donnellan once threw a boomerang 377 feet, a distance longer than a football field. A boomerang uses gravity and air resistance to aid its flight. Guerrilla creativity uses other weapons to aid its flight. The most important of those weapons is a meme. But it's hardly the only weapon you should be using. Single-weapon marketing has nothing to aid its flight.

That's why one of the key factors in marketing today is integration of all your marketing with your meme. Integrated marketing gives your campaign a life of its own.

For example, a direct-mail campaign, even with a powerful meme, can go only so far. But if during that campaign your prospects read articles about you and see your meme in the newspaper, if they're invited to a special event you're sponsoring and see that meme again, if they hear you interviewed on a radio talk show and hear you speak your meme, if they see your ads, all containing your meme, if they read that you'll be giving a talk somewhere — and somehow manage to remember your meme — that's when your direct-mail campaign becomes infused with the physics of the boomerang and flies much further than it would ordinarily.

If your TV spots are saying one thing, your designer came up with print ads that say something else, your Web site is off on a third tangent, and your direct mail is doing its own thing — that kind of nonguerrilla creativity is not integrated and it will not work. To make these well-selected weapons operational, they all must be featuring the same meme, pulling in the same direction, saying virtually the same thing, helping to clarify instead of confuse the consumer. Everything in the boomerang's flight is designed for maximum airtime — and accuracy.

An integrated solution to a marketing problem begins with close inspection of yourself, your target audience, and your marketing environment. Your prospect's state of mind, life-style, and media usage are the best clues you have to discovering which combination of tactics and weaponry will bring about maximum results.

Every element of your mix should spring from and reinforce the single strategic meme behind the campaign. Divergent approaches baffle the prospect and put a drag on the thrust of your campaign. Without the integration provided by your meme, you've got a shapeless stick doing battle for you. With a meme, you've got a sleek, aerodynamic flying machine.

Integrated marketing with a meme as the common thread is the hallmark of the present and future. Great news for guerrillas, but hardly what award-lovers living in the past want to hear.

Should you use an advertising agency?

It may be that rather than allow your own creative juices to flow, you want to have the creative juices of an advertising agency flowing for you. One of the easiest ways to lose a lot of money, however, is to select the wrong advertising agency. It completely wastes your investment, raises false hopes, and increases your frustration. And yet the wrong ad agencies are chosen all the time.

Companies select the wrong agency because they are wooed by razzle-dazzle and dynamic presentations, by big names and clever ideas — rather than by a solid grasp of the true purpose of advertising. That purpose is to generate profits for your company — and nothing else. That purpose is achieved when you realize that advertising is simply a fancy word for selling.

It is important to realize that advertising agencies are mis-named in the current economic environment. Instead of focus-ing on advertising, a truly effective ad agency focuses on mar-keting and knows that advertising is only one of the many forms of marketing. Beware of the ad agency that speaks only of advertising and neglects the many other functions of market-ing. Because they are advertising agencies, they see their mis-sion as advertising, but you must keep in mind that advertising is only part of the process of generating profits for yourself. I've never heard of an advertising agency that specializes in memes, but you can expect such agencies to rise to the fore now that we're learning of the immense power of memes.

Selecting an agency means selecting a member of your team — and teaming up is what you'll do. You should be prepared to give as much as you get and to view the agency as a valued member of your marketing team, not simply a company that creates great advertising on its own.

The benefit of a good agency

A solid advertising agency can make your life a lot easier and risk-free. It should view your business from your stand-point, not its own. Beware of the advertising agency that speaks proudly of the awards it has won. Keep your radar attuned to the agency that speaks instead of the profitability and growth it has achieved for its past and current clients. If you hear an agency even mention memes, lean forward and pay close atten-tion.

As a rule, the longer the agency has served its current clients, the better prepared it will be to help your company in its quest for success. Great advertising agencies become great because their clients have grown and prospered. Ideally, the agency that you select should be your agency for the next fifty years or more, and it will grow by helping you grow.

You must view your task as helping the ad agency you select. Unfortunately, many companies set up an adversarial relationship, gently criticizing the agency's ideas and work, stoning it to death with popcorn, as one agency president with popcorn scars once said.

Your most significant contributions will come in the form of data and judgment. Supply data that advertising agencies can be creative about — remembering that the true definition of creativity is something that generates profits for your company. Use clear judgment in recognizing who works as the advertising professional and who makes the products and services to be advertised and marketed. Each has his own expertise. Ask the ad agency staff whether they know about memes, and if they don't, explain memes to them. Don't forget that many of them operate in ivory towers, far removed from the new recognition of memes.

Big names and small businesses

I've spent many years working for advertising agencies worldwide, and I've spent even more years servicing clients who hire agencies. So I've had the opportunity to view advertising from both sides of the fence. Leaning on that experience, I urge you not to select a big-name advertising agency if you're a small-name company.

The chiefs of those large agencies will make a presentation that will win your heart — and your business. But they will not be the people who work on your business. Big agencies often assign the work to neophytes. They don't see the need to have their most fertile minds and most highly paid employees helping your growing company when they could be helping their largest clients grow even larger. Remember that ad agencies are as profit-minded as you are, but frequently it is their own profits on which they concentrate. Keep in mind that they earn enormous commissions by placing advertising for their large clients.

Rule of thumb for guerrillas

A rule of thumb: the smaller your business, the smaller an ad agency you should seek. The larger your company, the more services you'll need. A giant advertiser recently moved some of its business from its extremely successful agency in a small city in the United States to a far larger agency in a larger city — because the larger agency had more global services and this advertiser was seriously thinking globally. Global matters might not influence your own decision in an agency. Its services and the quality of the people who will be doing the work on your business should be your prime considerations.

Choosing an ad agency: ten questions to ask

Before you go about the difficult task of choosing an ad agency, you should ask yourself ten questions:

1. *What do we need from an agency — help in planning, researching, creating, producing, picking media, all of these, or none of these?* If you don't have a need, it may

be that you don't need an agency and can function with the services of a freelancer. Or even do it all by yourself.

2. *Should the ad agency handle the media buying, will we do that ourselves, or should we use a media-buying service?* Just because the agency offers it doesn't mean you have to use it.

3. *Will the agency be compensated solely by the commission it earns on the media it purchases and the added commission it earns on production, or will it require a flat fee that includes all services?* I've never heard of a surgeon charging a commission on the cost of the operating room. But watch out for hourly fees. Agencies often nearly bankrupt companies with these, and not on purpose. I recommend getting a monthly estimate on them. Or I'd try to avoid them entirely by means of a flat fee covering specific projects.

4. *Are we picking an agency because we want a specific kind of advertising campaign or because it's the best agency?* Beware of agencies that specialize in one kind of advertising. Your company isn't like the others for which they have created advertising. You're different, and your ads should reflect that.

5. *How important is it that we have regular and unlimited access to the president of the agency we select?* If you get to see her and she's not involved with your account regularly, you may be wasting your time and money. If you get to see someone from one management layer down and that person lives and breathes your business, the president means little to you.

6. *Does the agency have quantifiable prowess in direct marketing and the Internet, since that so closely ties in with marketing?* If the answer is no, go directly to the next agency. Direct marketing and the Internet are integral parts of marketing, and their importance is growing every day.

7. *Do we require an agency to handle our existing advertising only or our new product launches and grand openings as well?* The correct response is, "Everything." How adept is the agency at introducing new products, and does it have access to first-rate public relations services? The two correct answers are "great" and "of course."

8. *Does the location of the ad agency matter to us?* In these days of e-mail, Web sites, faxes, cellular phones, and satellite transmission, location is less important than ever. Nonetheless, personal contact is the best form of communication. Will you miss it if you don't get it?

9. *Although we have the ultimate say-so in what advertising runs, who will really be in charge of all advertising decisions — someone at our place or someone at the agency? Do we respect that person?*

10. I've saved the best for last: *Do we love both the work done by the agency and the results it has achieved? Do we like the people? Do we trust them? Are they more concerned with awards or sales?* Subtract ten points for everything they say about awards instead of profits. I have won many international advertising awards, but I

am far more proud of the profits my clients have earned. Awards don't pay the bills.

Five things to look for in an advertising agency

Make your ad agency selection, if you decide you need one, based on the needs of the twenty-first century guerrilla.

1. *Be certain that the ad agency realizes that advertising is only a small portion of marketing.* The agency must demonstrate that it knows there are many more marketing weapons to utilize and that it is capable of using or directing the use of all of the appropriate ones in your potential marketing arsenal. Guerrilla businesses deserve guerrilla advertising agencies. Don't settle for less.

2. *Ascertain that your account will be considered important, special, and deserving of the agency's top talent.* Be sure you meet and talk to the people who will actually be doing your advertising — creative, media, research, the whole works. See what else the creative people have created. Ask about the results. Avoid agency figureheads and get to know the troops who will be serving on your front line. Is the chemistry right between you? Don't underestimate the immense power of good chemistry.

3. *Be sure your agency understands your company's objectives and considers them reasonable.* This understanding will be reflected in the agency's creation of your marketing and advertising strategy. If it's missing, look elsewhere.

4. *Check to see that the people who will be working on your account have the right credentials, experience, and attitude.* Make sure they are good listeners. If they haven't worked on a

business like yours, don't worry. They can learn about it. Just make sure that they understand the critical relationship between profitability and creativity. If it doesn't help you earn profits, it's not creative.

5. *Be positive that the agency has a knowledge of your business, an interest in your business, and a knowledge of the competitive situation.* The agency need not be experienced at working for companies in an industry such as yours, but it should have studied your business enough to have more than a nodding acquaintance with both your company and your industry. If the agency has done its homework by the time it presents to you, it'll have these things. If not, you're not interested.

If you do need an advertising agency, be sure to look at the ads and other marketing materials that a prospective agency has created: memes, theme lines, logos, signs, telemarketing scripts, brochures, videos, catalogs, newsletters, Web sites, direct-mail letters, postcards, posters, even postcard mailers.

The best advertising agencies

The best advertising agencies have grown from the growth of their clients and their ever-increasing marketing investments. This is a better benchmark than growth derived from new clients attracted by the work they have done for other clients. Such agencies are hard to find, but the search will be worth your time.

Ask a prospective advertising agency to make a presentation to you, but don't ask the agency to spend a lot of money doing so. Listen to the agency people's words: do they talk more about you than about themselves? Be aware of the emphasis they place on strategy, for that strategy is crucial to you. See whether they know how advertising fits into the overall marketing mix, and beware if they speak only about advertising and hardly at all about marketing.

You must do all in your power to know the difference between clever advertising and effective advertising. Be wary of the agency that relies too much on the use of humor, for humor, as we've learned, is often the enemy of effective advertising.

Be sure that your advertising agency understands the crucial necessity for follow-up, that it's abreast of the growth of online marketing and the new opportunities that offers, and that it is up-to-date but not too far in advance of society.

Think of selecting an agency the same way you'd think about selecting a mate to marry. The best relationships are long-term. Each party likes the other and is completely honest. Their love is measured by their desire to make each other happy — not just with words but with words and deeds combined. They are focused more on each other than on themselves. They are willing to do the hard work to handle bumps in the road because they have so clear a vision of the future.

Each party probably played the field at first, and then, after meeting each other and falling in love, they learned about each other before they married. Selecting an agency properly will probably require that you do the same. Make sure you and the agency you select have the same priorities so that there are no surprises.

You can learn about an agency not only through its presentation but also by walking around the agency offices, looking at its work in progress for other clients and seeing for yourself the agency's passion and enthusiasm for creating advertising that works.

What to be aware of

Be especially aware of advertising the agency has created that's been running for a long time — a sure sign that it is successful. Be sure the agency is willing to experiment and test out ideas for creating timeless materials. Watch out if it creates parasite advertising — the kind in which cleverness, jokes, and special effects draw attention away from your offering.

Great advertising is the kind that forgets the advertising and ensures that the product or service is the star of the ad or commercial. Great advertising agencies produce advertising that creates a desire to buy. Advertising is not supposed to make people say, "What wonderful advertising!" Instead, it is supposed to make people say, "I want that product."

Advertising creativity comes from knowledge. The more knowledge the agency possesses, the more creative it can be. A powerful agency asks questions, listens to answers, engages in tireless research, and never stops learning.

Can your advertising agency help you engage in fusion marketing arrangements with others — combining marketing efforts to reach more people but saving money by sharing the cost? A top agency is not guided by its own corporate ego but by its desire to help you achieve your goals. It uses technology to the utmost but does not rely too much on technology. Its advertising begins with your offering and the reason you are in business in the first place — not with a snappy jingle or a dazzling graphic approach.

Operating without an ad agency

With this new wisdom about what advertising agencies ought to offer, many businesses are now functioning very well, thank you, without standard ad agencies. Valuable information about marketing has never been as abundant, primarily owing to the Internet.

The result of all this has been the growth of the guerrilla, the executive who brings talent and judgment to many marketing areas and who understands the striking power of a meme. These people aren't scared of marketing or intimated by media, and they know how to do research, realize the abundance of free weapons, and believe as fervently in operating from a plan as they do in keeping everything simple.

They're fascinated with online marketing, love the accountability of direct marketing, and are as intrigued with newsletters and customer follow-up as they are with TV. The very thought of a meme excites them beyond words.

For years, even decades, they've been scouring the body of marketing knowledge for some common denominator of greatness, for some simple and inexpensive way to break free of the chaos in marketing, for an understandable, nontrendy way to communicate their message.

They, and possibly you, not only need a meme but want a meme, crave a meme, yes, even lust for a meme. It's a new century, and there's a new kind of jungle out there. New weapons will be needed. Memes are hardly new, having been around since the dawn of humankind. But the intentional use of memes in marketing is new. A meme for your company is new.

Three roads to take

Right now, after having inflicted all this information on you, I feel compelled to alert you to the crossroads at which you stand. One road leads to passing on the idea of creating a meme for your business for now, much as many companies passed on the idea of marketing online when it first became available. Inaction is frequently the action of the majority.

A second road leads to knowing that you're going to need a meme for your business one of these days, but for now you'll continue to market without one. The largest group of the minority opts for waiting a bit before taking action.

The third road leads to taking on the task of creating a meme right this moment. The very smallest group is that small band of people who take action, who travel down the third road.

I'd love to provide you with a pen and paper right now so that I could help you get started. I'm tempted to ask you to take the pen you have with you and draw or write your meme inside the cover of this book. But I don't want to upset any librarians, the living search engines who are one of America's great untapped resources.

The third road is the guerrilla route. Guerrillas don't look forward to the meme they're going to create but look back with satisfaction on the meme they've had ever since they learned of memes in marketing, the one that helped them reduce their marketing budget while increasing their profits.

The glory of a meme

Because a meme in marketing is such a fresh idea, and because memes come from a scientific field, some people may be apprehensive about the complexity of negotiating this new terrain.

The glory of a meme is not in its complexity, however, but in its ability to compress complex information and make it extraordinarily simple. In fact, the most winning characteristic of a meme is its compression ability. Complicated ideas such as religion, faith, life after death, heaven, hell, Democrats, Republicans, politics, superstition, time, space, geographical boundaries, right and left, right and wrong, capitalism, cults, ceremonies, hygiene, fashion, music, currency, design, sports, and love are represented by memes. Hardly new, these memes have been part of nature and evolution since the beginning of mankind. They are the basis for language and all human communication.

Memes shape our attitudes and belief patterns. They influence our behavior. The book *Spiral Dynamics* by Don Beck and Christopher Cowan tells us that they reveal the hidden codes that shape human nature, create global diversities, and drive evolutionary change. Yet, as a force in marketing, memes are on the cutting edge. That's where guerrillas feel most comfortable.

Memes also function best in the present moment, which is when they accomplish the lion's share of their work. In this moment is when they begin to create the meme that will be as timeless as the ones that have been with us since the beginnings of recorded time.

Just as Winston Churchill used a meme when he raised his hand and spread two of his fingers in a "V" for victory, you will do the same when you gain the upper ground in the battle for the minds of your prospects by using your own meme.

The centerpiece of guerrilla creativity

Guerrilla creativity begins, is centered on, and ends with a meme.

The Internet was developed for military use and is now recognized as the next battleground for marketing. In the same way, memes were discovered in a genetics setting and now are recognized as the most powerful armament for victory on that battleground — and many others.

The alert entrepreneur who embraces the idea of enlisting a meme for marketing, then is the first to create and activate that meme, will be the victor.

To the victor go the customers. To the victor go the profits.

Sources

Ayling, Geoff. *Rapid Response Advertising.* Warriewood, Australia: Business and Professional Publishing, 1998.

Beck, Don, and Christopher Cowan. *Spiral Dynamics.* Malden, Mass.: Blackwell, 1995.

Brin, David. "The New Meme." Kspace.com: Kaleidospace, 1993.

Dawkins, Richard. *The Selfish Gene.* New York: Oxford University Press, 1976.

Deep, Sam, and Lyle Sussman. *Close the Deal: Smart Moves for Selling.* Cambridge, Mass.: Perseus, 1999.

Godin, Seth. *Permission Marketing.* New York: Simon & Schuster, 1999.

———. *Unleashing the Ideavirus.* New York: Simon & Schuster, 2001.

Goodrum, Charles, and Helen Dalrymple. *Advertising in America: The First 200 Years.* New York: Harry N. Abrams, 1990.

Reeves, Rosser. *Reality in Advertising.* New York: Alfred A. Knopf, 1981.

Ries, Al, and Jack Trout. *Positioning: The Battle for Your Mind.* New York: McGraw-Hill Professional Book Group, 2001.

Shlain, Leonard. *The Alphabet Versus the Goddess: The Conflict Between Word and Image.* New York: Penguin Putnam, 1998.

Williams, Roy H. *Secret Formulas of the Wizard of Ads.* Austin, Tex.: Bard Press, 1999.

Index

Continue Your Guerrilla Training with the *Guerrilla Marketing Newsletter*

Published continuously since 1986, the *Guerrilla Marketing Newsletter* provides you with state-of-the-moment insights to maximize the profits you can obtain through marketing. The newsletter is written to furnish you with the cream of the new guerrilla marketing information from around the world, along with new perspectives on existing wisdom about marketing. It is filled with practical advice, the latest research, upcoming trends, and brand-new marketing techniques — all designed to pay off in profits to you.

A yearly subscription costs $59 for six issues.

All subscribers are given this unique guarantee. If you aren't convinced after examining your first issue for thirty days that the newsletter will raise your profits, your subscription fee will be refunded — along with $2 just for trying.

To subscribe and get a free brochure, call, write, or e-mail us at:

> Guerrilla Marketing International
> 260 Cascade Drive, PO Box 1336
> Mill Valley, CA 94912
> 1-800-748-6444
> E-mail: GM INTL@aol.com

If you're online, check my Guerrilla Marketing Online Web site at **www.jayconradlevinson.com.** And receive continuing support with the Guerrilla Marketing Coaching Program. Now you can have your own personal guerrilla marketing coach. Just pick up the phone right in your own office — call from anywhere in the world — and engage in live telephone communication with Jay Levinson as you give wings to your plans.

For more information, visit **www.gmarketingcoach.com** or call 1-312-440-0815.

Get the Complete
GUERRILLA ARSENAL!

THE WAY OF THE GUERRILLA
Achieving Success and Balance as an Entrepreneur
in the 21st Century

An invaluable blueprint for future business success, *The Way of the Guerrilla* includes advice on everything from preparing a focused mission statement to sustaining one's passion for work. Entrepreneurs will discover the means to achieving emotional and financial success.

0-395-92478-2, $13.00

GUERRILLA MARKETING ONLINE
The Entrepreneur's Guide to Earning Profits on
the Internet, Second Edition

From building and maintaining a Web site to creating an online catalog and encouraging users to shop on the Net, Jay Levinson and computer book author Charles Rubin teach entrepreneurs what they need to know to become Internet marketing experts.

0-395-86061-X, $ 14.00

GUERRILLA MARKETING ONLINE WEAPONS
100 Low-Cost, High-Impact Weapons for Online
Profits and Prosperity

From e-mail addresses and signatures to storefronts, feedback mechanisms, electronic catalogs, and press kits, Levinson and Rubin's weapons will help any business define, refine, and post its message online with ease.

0-395-77019-X, $14.00

GUERRILLA MARKETING FOR THE
HOME-BASED BUSINESS

Using case studies, anecdotes, illustrations, and examples, guerrilla marketing gurus Jay Levinson and Seth Godin present practical, accessible, and inspirational marketing advice and the most effective marketing tools for America's fastest-growing business segment.

0-395-74283-8, $13.00

THE GUERRILLA MARKETING HANDBOOK

An essential companion to *Guerrilla Marketing,* this practical guide offers thousands of contacts, ideas, and examples that will help transform plans into specific actions, turning any business into a marketing powerhouse.

0-395-70013-2, $18.00

GUERRILLA ADVERTISING
Cost-Effective Tactics for Small-Business Success

Full of anecdotes about past and current advertising successes and failures, *Guerrilla Advertising* entertains as it teaches the nuts and bolts of advertising for small businesses.

0-395-68718-7, $ 13.00

GUERRILLA MARKETING EXCELLENCE
The 50 Golden Rules for Small-Business Success

Outlining 50 basic truths that can make or break your company, *Guerrilla Marketing Excellence* takes readers beyond do-it-yourself marketing guides, explaining not just how to market but how to market with excellence.

0-395-60844-9, $14.00

GUERRILLA FINANCING
Alternative Techniques to Finance Any Small Business

The ultimate sourcebook for finance, *Guerrilla Financing* is the first book to describe in detail the many traditional and alternative sources of funding available for small and medium-size businesses.

0-395-52264-1, $14.00

GUERRILLA SELLING
Unconventional Weapons and Tactics for Increasing Your Sales

Today's increasingly competitive business environment requires new skills and commitment from salespeople. *Guerrilla Selling* presents unconventional selling tactics that are essential for success.

0-395-57820-5, $13.00

GUERRILLA MARKETING ATTACK
New Strategies, Tactics, and Weapons for Winning Big Profits

Guerrilla Marketing Attack explains how to avoid running out of fuel by maximizing limited start-up resources and turning prospects into customers and investments into profits.

0-395-50220-9, $13.00

GUERRILLA CREATIVITY

The guru of guerrilla marketing unveils his methods of optimizing originality and creativity for successful marketing. Levinson focuses on memes, simple symbols that convey complex ideas — how to generate them and how to disseminate them.

0-618-10468-2, $14.00

These books are available through bookstores or directly through Houghton Mifflin customer service at 1-800-225-3362.

Visit our Web sites at www.houghtonmifflinbooks.com and www.jayconradlevinson.com.